WORKING WITH THE REGISTRY USING C#.NET

Part 1

Richard Edwards

INTRODUCTIONS ARE IN ORDER

Why should you buy this book?

Imagine, for a moment, that you have just been told that one of your team members just installed an application that has caused a $2,000,000 profit per hour server to crash.

I'm sure the chaos about you is similar to someone yelling fire as the place fills up with smoke and there are no visible exits. Everyone is worried that their jobs are on the line.

It seems like everyone has tried to get that remotely run server to come back to life. There's even talk of rebooting the machine combined with the concern that control of the machine could be lost should they decide to go that way.

Since more than one person can log onto that server, you log in and start doing some checking. Seems you're the only one left in the office that isn't crowded around the server.

You are also smart enough to take a registry snapshot of the server and the program you built which compares the current registry settings on the server verses what is there shows you where the server's issue is.

The keys that need to be put pack into the registry are silently added and IIS gets a restart. All of a sudden, as though sheer will power from the people around the computer screen made it happen, the server springs back to live and the tension in the room vaporizes.

So, what was the problem? The problem was the developer pushed a newer type library over to the server. The only person who could run the program as the dev. So, as soon as the program was activated – which would happen as soon as the default webpage was requested and the new developer's permissions were invoked, IIS would crash.

Sound farfetched? Think again. While not fixing a server down scenario, I did fix a similar issue on a server where the developers credentials stopped his program from working.

Worked great on his development machine because it was his development machine but failed when launched on the server. When we compared the permissions on a known type library that worked, once the permissions were duplicated over to the developer's type library, the program began to work the way it was designed.

Now, I'm not telling you it is okay to start fiddling around with the security settings in the registry and certainly not on a live server. What I am saying is if you know the registry as I do and know what you're doing, then someday, perhaps, fixing an issue like this might be on your radar.

In the meantime, you might want to try learning how you can use your coding skills and the examples in this book to learn about what you can find in it and do it in such a way that you're just looking and not changing anything in the process.

Am I a registry expert? A lot yes and a little no. I have a lot of respect for the registry and love finding new ways to work with it. But I wouldn't exactly call myself an expert. I simply know what to do to resolve issues.

But I will say this in my defense of not wearing a registry expert badge, I've worked with the registry's APIs while working at Microsoft and working the phones solving Visual Basic Enterprise level support issues.

As a matter of fact, while working for Microsoft Technical Support, when the .Net Framework was first introduced, I started learning how to program in C#.Net and C++.Net using the registry code that was suggested for VB.Net and turned it into C#.Net and C++.Net code.

In-other-words, I have a ton of code to share with you that uses C#.Net. This includes creating remote and local connections, working with both the 32-bit and the 64-bit versions of the registry and manipulating the code to look for specific registry keys and values that you can use as reusable code.

WHAT HAPPENED TO:

WHY DID THIS HAPPEN

AND WHEN DID IT

START?

Many things happen based on an event. A new piece of software, an update, and even a hardware change can be factors that create an event that needs immediate attention or money is lost and people's jobs are at stake.

Working with the registry has gotten a lot easier. Seemed like when you wanted to work the registry you more concerned about the IDE blue screening for no other reason that it could. Then I had to load in a text file. Select constants and then the APIs themselves. The constants looked like this:

```
Public Const HKEY_CLASSES_ROOT = &H80000000
Public Const HKEY_CURRENT_CONFIG = &H80000005
Public Const HKEY_CURRENT_USER = &H80000001
Public Const HKEY_DYN_DATA = &H80000006
Public Const HKEY_LOCAL_MACHINE = &H80000002
Public Const HKEY_PERFORMANCE_DATA = &H80000004
Public Const HKEY_USERS = &H80000003
```

Then, I had to find the registry APIs:

Declare Function RegOpenKey Lib "advapi32.dll" Alias "RegOpenKeyA" (ByVal hKey As Long, ByVal lpSubKey As String, phkResult As Long) As Long

Declare Function RegEnumKey Lib "advapi32.dll" Alias "RegEnumKeyA" (ByVal hKey As Long, ByVal dwIndex As Long, ByVal lpName As String, ByVal cbName As Long) As Long

Declare Function RegEnumValue Lib "advapi32.dll" Alias "RegEnumValueA" (ByVal hKey As Long, ByVal dwIndex As Long, ByVal lpValueName As String, lpcbValueName As Long, lpReserved As Long, lpType As Long, lpData As Byte, lpcbData As Long) As Long

As you can pretty well image this wasn't the easiest stuff to work with.

```vbnet
Imports System.Text

Public Class Form1

    Public Const HKEY_CLASSES_ROOT = &H80000000
    Public Const HKEY_CURRENT_CONFIG = &H80000005
    Public Const HKEY_CURRENT_USER = &H80000001

    Public Const HKEY_DYN_DATA = &H80000006
    Public Const HKEY_LOCAL_MACHINE = &H80000002
    Public Const HKEY_PERFORMANCE_DATA = &H80000004
    Public Const HKEY_USERS = &H80000003

    Dim sb As StringBuilder = New StringBuilder(255)

    Declare Function RegOpenKey Lib "advapi32.dll" Alias "RegOpenKeyA" (ByVal hKey As Integer, ByVal lpSubKey As String, ByRef phkResult As Integer) As Integer
    Declare Function RegEnumKey Lib "advapi32.dll" Alias "RegEnumKeyA" (ByVal hKey As Integer, ByVal dwIndex As Integer, ByVal lpName As StringBuilder, ByVal cbName As Integer) As Integer

    Private Sub Form1_Load(ByVal sender As System.Object, ByVal e As System.EventArgs) Handles MyBase.Load


        Dim OpenResult As Integer = 0
        Dim iret As Integer = RegOpenKey(HKEY_LOCAL_MACHINE, "SOFTWARE\WOW6432Node\Classes\CLSID", OpenResult)
        Dim iret1 As Integer = 0
        Dim v As Integer = 0
        While iret1 = 0
            iret1 = RegEnumKey(OpenResult, v, sb, 255)
            If Mid(sb.ToString, 1, 1) = "{" Then
                ListBox1.Items.Add(sb.ToString())
```

```
        End If
        v = v + 1
    End While

  End Sub

End Class
```

Which produced this:

🖳 Form1

{00000010-0000-0010-8000-00AA006D2EA4}
{00000011-0000-0010-8000-00AA006D2EA4}
{00000013-0000-0010-8000-00AA006D2EA4}
{00000014-0000-0010-8000-00AA006D2EA4}
{00000015-0000-0010-8000-00AA006D2EA4}
{00000016-0000-0010-8000-00AA006D2EA4}
{00000017-0000-0010-8000-00AA006D2EA4}
{00000018-0000-0010-8000-00AA006D2EA4}
{00000019-0000-0010-8000-00AA006D2EA4}
{0000002F-0000-0000-C000-000000000046}
{00000100-0000-0010-8000-00AA006D2EA4}
{00000101-0000-0010-8000-00AA006D2EA4}
{00000103-0000-0010-8000-00AA006D2EA4}
{00000104-0000-0010-8000-00AA006D2EA4}
{00000105-0000-0010-8000-00AA006D2EA4}
{00000106-0000-0010-8000-00AA006D2EA4}
{00000107-0000-0010-8000-00AA006D2EA4}
{00000108-0000-0010-8000-00AA006D2EA4}
{00000109-0000-0010-8000-00AA006D2EA4}
{00000300-0000-0000-C000-000000000046}
{00000301-A8F2-4877-BA0A-FD2B6645FB94}
{00000303-0000-0000-C000-000000000046}
{00000304-0000-0000-C000-000000000046}
{00000305-0000-0000-C000-000000000046}
{00000306-0000-0000-C000-000000000046}
{00000308-0000-0000-C000-000000000046}
{00000309-0000-0000-C000-000000000046}
{0000030B-0000-0000-C000-000000000046}

In c#.Net, I simply do this to do the same thing:

```csharp
using System;
using System.Collections.Generic;
using System.ComponentModel;
using System.Data;
using System.Drawing;
using System.Linq;
using System.Text;
using System.Windows.Forms;
using Microsoft.Win32;
namespace WindowsFormsApplication1
{
    public partial class Form1 : Form
    {
        public Form1()
        {
            InitializeComponent();
        }

        private void Form1_Load(object sender, EventArgs e)
        {
            string[] names =
Registry.LocalMachine.OpenSubKey("Software\\WOW6432Node\\Classes\\C
LSID").GetSubKeyNames();

            foreach (string n in names)
            {
                if (n.Substring(0, 1) == "{")
                {
                    listBox1.Items.Add(n);
                }
            }
        }
    }
}
```
The results are the same.

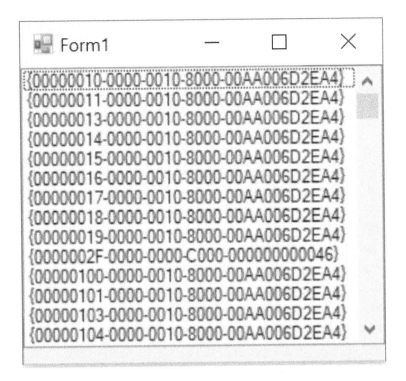

Was that easy or what? All the registry calls have been placed into a wrapper around the same APIs I would normally have to add and modify to make them work. Including values and value names.

So, what does this code do? Well, first, it connects to the registry and goes to the 32-bit version of Software\\Classes\\CLSID registry subkeys. But we're being very specific and adding: WOW6432Node right after the Software key. Anything we add at this point is called a sub key.

Anyway, after we've established where we want to go in the registry, we have the ability to enumerate through what sub keys or values are registered there. In this particular case, I want to enumerate through all the subkeys and add to that the key I'm looking for.

WHAT GOOD ARE THE REGISTRY ENTRIES IF I CAN'T GET WHAT I WANT FROM THEM?

Which means I have a reason for going to the CLSID subkey.

The CLSID subkey exposes all of the ClassIDs – GUIDS with curly brackets around them and provides hints on what each one does. For as long as I can remember, the trademark of ADO has been the use of the same build machine. The GUIDS generated by that machine end in 6D2EA4 and have remained the same since 1996.

For historical purposes, the registry's sections was originally called a hive. I think it was called that because the programmer who wrote the code to work with it, was stung by a bee while coming to work. And I'm pretty sure, after working with the registry, he realized the relationship. One wrong key deleted and you're rebuilding the machine.

Also, the purpose of the registry originally was to have one place where all the program information – what we used to call ini files – can be stored. Well, when COM came along, AppIDs, ClassIDs, Interfaces, ProgIDs, VersionIndependentProgIDs and Type Libraries found their home in the registry.

Originally, these were found in HKEY_CLASSES_ROOT and the code to go through them looked a little like this:

```
using System;
using System.Collections.Generic;
using System.Linq;
using System.Text;
using Microsoft.Win32;
namespace ListRegistryEntries
{
    class clsClassesRoot
    {
        public System.String[] Get_Root_Names()
        {
            String[] names;
```

```csharp
        names = Registry.ClassesRoot.GetSubKeyNames();

        return names;
    }
    public System.Collections.Generic.Dictionary<string,
string> Get_ProgIDs(System.String[] ns)
    {
        System.Collections.Generic.Dictionary<string, string>
pidy = new System.Collections.Generic.Dictionary<string,
string>();

        foreach (System.String n1 in ns)
        {
            RegistryKey regkey =
Registry.ClassesRoot.OpenSubKey(n1 + "\\CLSID");
            if (regkey != null)
            {
                try
                {
                    System.String s1 = n1;
                    System.String s2 =
regkey.GetValue("").ToString();
                    pidy.Add(s1, s2);
                }
                catch (Exception ex)
                {

                }
            }
        }
        return pidy;
    }
```

Up to this point, everything worked just fine. But when I try to check for the object being a control or and OLE DB Provider, these routines fail. This is something that never happened before the arrival of 64-bit operating systems.

```csharp
        public System.Collections.Generic.Dictionary<string,
string> Get_Filtered_ProgIDs(System.String[] ns)
        {
```

```csharp
            System.Collections.Generic.Dictionary<string, string>
pidy = new System.Collections.Generic.Dictionary<string,
string>();


            foreach (System.String n1 in ns)
            {
                RegistryKey regkey =
Registry.ClassesRoot.OpenSubKey(n1 + "\\CLSID");
                if (regkey != null)
                {
                    try
                    {
                        System.String s1 = n1;
                        System.String s2 =
regkey.GetValue("").ToString();
                        RegistryKey regkey1 =
Registry.ClassesRoot.OpenSubKey("CLSID\\" + s2 + "\\Control");
                        if(regkey1 == null)
                        {
                            RegistryKey regkey2 =
Registry.ClassesRoot.OpenSubKey("CLSID\\" + s2 + "\\OLE DB
Provider");

                            if (regkey2 == null)
                            {

                                pidy.Add(s1, s2);
                            }
                        }

                    }
                    catch (Exception ex)
                    {

                    }
                }
            }
            return pidy;
        }
    }
}
```

So, how am I going to fix it? Well, first, without the filtering, I get a total of 3,260 entries. The adjusted code below generates 2, 705 entries.

```csharp
        public System.Collections.Generic.Dictionary<string,
string> Get_Filtered_ProgIDs(System.String[] ns)
        {
            System.Collections.Generic.Dictionary<string, string>
pidy = new System.Collections.Generic.Dictionary<string,
string>();


            foreach (System.String n1 in ns)
            {
                RegistryKey regkey =
Registry.ClassesRoot.OpenSubKey(n1 + "\\CLSID");
                if (regkey != null)
                {

                    String cat =
(System.String)regkey.GetValue("");
                    RegistryKey reg =
Registry.LocalMachine.OpenSubKey("Software\\WOW6432Node\\Classes\
\CLSID\\" + cat);
                    if (reg != null)
                    {
                        RegistryKey regkey1 =
Registry.LocalMachine.OpenSubKey("Software\\WOW6432Node\\Classes\
\CLSID\\" + cat + "\\Control");
                        if (regkey1 == null)
                        {
                            RegistryKey regkey2 =
Registry.LocalMachine.OpenSubKey("Software\\WOW6432Node\\Classes\
\CLSID\\" + cat + "\\HTMLControl");
                            if (regkey2 == null)
                            {
                                RegistryKey regkey3 =
Registry.LocalMachine.OpenSubKey("Software\\WOW6432Node\\Classes\
\CLSID\\" + cat + "\\OLE DB Provider");
                                if (regkey3 == null)
                                {
                                    System.String s1 = n1;
                                    System.String s2 = cat;
                                    pidy.Add(s1, s2);
                                }
                            }
                        }
                    }
```

```
                }
                else
                {
                    String cat1 =
(System.String)regkey.GetValue("");
                        RegistryKey reg1 =
Registry.ClassesRoot.OpenSubKey("CLSID\\" + cat1);
                    if (reg1 != null)
                    {
                        RegistryKey regkey11 =
Registry.ClassesRoot.OpenSubKey("CLSID\\" + cat1 + "\\Control");
                        if (regkey11 == null)
                        {
                            RegistryKey regkey22 =
Registry.ClassesRoot.OpenSubKey("CLSID\\" + cat1 +
"\\HTMLControl");

                            if (regkey22 == null)
                            {
                                RegistryKey regkey33 =
Registry.ClassesRoot.OpenSubKey("CLSID\\" + cat1 + "\\OLE DB
Provider");

                                if (regkey33 == null)
                                {
                                    System.String s1 = n1;
                                    System.String s2 = cat1;
                                    pidy.Add(s1, s2);
                                }
                            }
                        }
                    }
                }
            }
        return pidy;
    }
```

This is some of the fastest code I've ever worked with. It is also a combination of three programs in one. If I was just looking for OLE DB Providers:

```
public System.Collections.Generic.Dictionary<string,
string> Get_Providers_From_ProgIDs(System.String[] ns)
    {
        System.Collections.Generic.Dictionary<string, string>
pidy = new System.Collections.Generic.Dictionary<string,
string>();
```

```csharp
foreach (System.String n1 in ns)
{
    RegistryKey regkey =
Registry.ClassesRoot.OpenSubKey(n1 + "\\CLSID");
    if (regkey != null)
    {

        String cat =
(System.String)regkey.GetValue("");
        RegistryKey reg =
Registry.LocalMachine.OpenSubKey("Software\\WOW6432Node\\Classes\
\CLSID\\" + cat);
        if (reg != null)
        {
            RegistryKey regkey1 =
Registry.LocalMachine.OpenSubKey("Software\\WOW6432Node\\Classes\
\CLSID\\" + cat + "\\Control");
            if (regkey1 == null)
            {
                RegistryKey regkey2 =
Registry.LocalMachine.OpenSubKey("Software\\WOW6432Node\\Classes\
\CLSID\\" + cat + "\\HTMLControl");
                if (regkey2 == null)
                {
                    RegistryKey regkey3 =
Registry.LocalMachine.OpenSubKey("Software\\WOW6432Node\\Classes\
\CLSID\\" + cat + "\\OLE DB Provider");
                    if (regkey3 != null)
                    {
                        System.String s1 = n1;
                        System.String s2 = cat;
                        pidy.Add(s1, s2);
                    }
                }
            }
        }
        else
        {
            String cat1 =
(System.String)regkey.GetValue("");
            RegistryKey reg1 =
Registry.ClassesRoot.OpenSubKey("CLSID\\" + cat1);
            if (reg1 != null)
```

```
                    {
                        RegistryKey regkey11 =
Registry.ClassesRoot.OpenSubKey("CLSID\\" + cat1 + "\\Control");
                        if (regkey11 == null)
                        {
                            RegistryKey regkey22 =
Registry.ClassesRoot.OpenSubKey("CLSID\\" + cat1 +
"\\HTMLControl");

                            if (regkey22 == null)
                            {
                                RegistryKey regkey33 =
Registry.ClassesRoot.OpenSubKey("CLSID\\" + cat1 + "\\OLE DB
Provider");

                                if (regkey33 != null)
                                {
                                    System.String s1 = n1;
                                    System.String s2 = cat1;
                                    pidy.Add(s1, s2);
                                }
                            }
                        }
                    }
                }
            }
        }
    }
    return pidy;
}
```

Output:

Same code but filtering for HTML Controls:

```csharp
        public System.Collections.Generic.Dictionary<string,
string> Get_HTMLCONTROLS_From_ProgIDs(System.String[] ns)
        {
            System.Collections.Generic.Dictionary<string, string>
pidy = new System.Collections.Generic.Dictionary<string,
string>();


            foreach (System.String n1 in ns)
            {
                RegistryKey regkey =
Registry.ClassesRoot.OpenSubKey(n1 + "\\CLSID");
                if (regkey != null)
                {

                    String cat =
(System.String)regkey.GetValue("");
                    RegistryKey reg =
Registry.LocalMachine.OpenSubKey("Software\\WOW6432Node\\Classes\
\CLSID\\" + cat);
                    if (reg != null)
                    {
                        RegistryKey regkey1 =
Registry.LocalMachine.OpenSubKey("Software\\WOW6432Node\\Classes\
\CLSID\\" + cat + "\\Control");
                        if (regkey1 == null)
                        {
                            RegistryKey regkey2 =
Registry.LocalMachine.OpenSubKey("Software\\WOW6432Node\\Classes\
\CLSID\\" + cat + "\\HTMLControl");
                            if (regkey2 != null)
                            {
                                System.String s1 = n1;
                                System.String s2 = cat;
                                pidy.Add(s1, s2);
                            }
                        }
                    }
                }
                else
                {
```

```csharp
                    String cat1 =
(System.String)regkey.GetValue("");
                    RegistryKey reg1 =
Registry.ClassesRoot.OpenSubKey("CLSID\\" + cat1);
                    if (reg1 != null)
                    {
                        RegistryKey regkey11 =
Registry.ClassesRoot.OpenSubKey("CLSID\\" + cat1 + "\\Control");
                        if (regkey11 == null)
                        {
                            RegistryKey regkey22 =
Registry.ClassesRoot.OpenSubKey("CLSID\\" + cat1 +
"\\HTMLControl");

                            if (regkey22 != null)
                            {
                                System.String s1 = n1;
                                System.String s2 = cat1;
                                pidy.Add(s1, s2);
                            }
                        }
                    }
                }
            }
            return pidy;
        }
```

The output:

ProgIDs	ClassIDs
Forms.HTML:Checkbox.1	{5512D116-5CC6-11CF-8D67-00AA00BDCE1D}
Forms.HTML:Hidden.1	{5512D11C-5CC6-11CF-8D67-00AA00BDCE1D}
Forms.HTML:Image.1	{5512D112-5CC6-11CF-8D67-00AA00BDCE1D}
Forms.HTML:Option.1	{5512D118-5CC6-11CF-8D67-00AA00BDCE1D}
Forms.HTML:Password.1	{5512D11E-5CC6-11CF-8D67-00AA00BDCE1D}
Forms.HTML:Reset.1	{5512D114-5CC6-11CF-8D67-00AA00BDCE1D}
Forms.HTML:Select.1	{5512D122-5CC6-11CF-8D67-00AA00BDCE1D}
Forms.HTML:Submitbutton.1	{5512D110-5CC6-11CF-8D67-00AA00BDCE1D}
Forms.HTML:Text.1	{5512D11A-5CC6-11CF-8D67-00AA00BDCE1D}
Forms.HTML:TextArea.1	{5512D124-5CC6-11CF-8D67-00AA00BDCE1D}

And Just Plain Controls:

```csharp
        public System.Collections.Generic.Dictionary<string,
string> Get_CONTROLS_From_ProgIDs(System.String[] ns)
        {
            System.Collections.Generic.Dictionary<string, string>
pidy = new System.Collections.Generic.Dictionary<string,
string>();


            foreach (System.String n1 in ns)
            {
                RegistryKey regkey =
Registry.ClassesRoot.OpenSubKey(n1 + "\\CLSID");
                if (regkey != null)
                {

                String cat =
(System.String)regkey.GetValue("");
                RegistryKey reg =
Registry.LocalMachine.OpenSubKey("Software\\WOW6432Node\\Classes\
\CLSID\\" + cat);
                if (reg != null)
                {
                    RegistryKey regkey1 =
Registry.LocalMachine.OpenSubKey("Software\\WOW6432Node\\Classes\
\CLSID\\" + cat + "\\Control");
                    if (regkey1 != null)
                    {
                        System.String s1 = n1;
                        System.String s2 = cat;
                        pidy.Add(s1, s2);
                    }
                }
                else
                {
                    String cat1 =
(System.String)regkey.GetValue("");
                    RegistryKey reg1 =
Registry.ClassesRoot.OpenSubKey("CLSID\\" + cat1);
                    if (reg1 != null)
                    {
```

```csharp
                        RegistryKey regkey11 =
Registry.ClassesRoot.OpenSubKey("CLSID\\" + cat1 + "\\Control");
                        if (regkey11 != null)
                        {
                                System.String s1 = n1;
                                System.String s2 = cat1;
                                pidy.Add(s1, s2);
                        }
                    }
                }
            }
        }
        return pidy;
    }
```

Output:

ProgIDs	ClassIDs
COMCTL.ImageListCtrl	{58DA8D8F-9D6A-101B-AFC0-4210102A8DA7}
COMCTL.ImageListCtrl.1	{58DA8D8F-9D6A-101B-AFC0-4210102A8DA7}
COMCTL.ListViewCtrl	{58DA8D8A-9D6A-101B-AFC0-4210102A8DA7}
COMCTL.ListViewCtrl.1	{58DA8D8A-9D6A-101B-AFC0-4210102A8DA7}
COMCTL.ProgCtrl	{0713E8D2-850A-101B-AFC0-4210102A8DA7}
COMCTL.ProgCtrl.1	{0713E8D2-850A-101B-AFC0-4210102A8DA7}
COMCTL.SBarCtrl	{6B7E638F-850A-101B-AFC0-4210102A8DA7}
COMCTL.SBarCtrl.1	{6B7E638F-850A-101B-AFC0-4210102A8DA7}
COMCTL.Slider	{373FF7F0-EB8B-11CD-8820-08002B2F4F5A}
COMCTL.Slider.1	{373FF7F0-EB8B-11CD-8820-08002B2F4F5A}
COMCTL.TabStrip	{9ED94440-E5E8-101B-B9B5-444553540000}
COMCTL.TabStrip.1	{9ED94440-E5E8-101B-B9B5-444553540000}
COMCTL.Toolbar	{612A8624-0FB3-11CE-8747-524153480004}
COMCTL.Toolbar.1	{612A8624-0FB3-11CE-8747-524153480004}
COMCTL.TreeCtrl	{0713E8A2-850A-101B-AFC0-4210102A8DA7}
COMCTL.TreeCtrl.1	{0713E8A2-850A-101B-AFC0-4210102A8DA7}
ComCtl2.Animation	{1E216240-1B7D-11CF-9D53-00AA003C9CB6}
ComCtl2.Animation.1	{1E216240-1B7D-11CF-9D53-00AA003C9CB6}
ComCtl2.UpDown	{026371C0-1B7C-11CF-9D53-00AA003C9CB6}
ComCtl2.UpDown.1	{026371C0-1B7C-11CF-9D53-00AA003C9CB6}
CommunicatorMeetingJoinAx.JoinManager	{10336656-40D7-4530-BCC0-86CD3D77D25F}
CommunicatorMeetingJoinAx.JoinManager.2	{10336656-40D7-4530-BCC0-86CD3D77D25F}
ConnectionDesigner.UserConnection	{FB079AE3-551B-11CF-A0BE-00AA0062BE57}
ConnectionDesigner.UserConnection.1	{FB079AE3-551B-11CF-A0BE-00AA0062BE57}
Control.TaskSymbol	{44F9A03B-A3EC-4F3B-9364-08E0007F21DF}

So, now, that we've been able to filter out only specific registry entries we want, let's try something different. This time we're simply going to a specific registry entry to discover if the what we are looking for is there or not.

NO BETTER TIME THAN NOW!

Let's suppose you want to know information about the installation of the operating system.

```csharp
using System;
using System.Collections.Generic;
using System.Linq;
using System.Text;
using Microsoft.Win32;
using Scripting;
namespace ListRegistryEntries
{
    class ClsOSInformation
    {
        public void Get_OS_Info(System.Windows.Forms.WebBrowser webBrowser1)
        {
            System.Collections.Generic.Dictionary<string, string> pidy = new System.Collections.Generic.Dictionary<string, string>();
            String[] names =
Registry.LocalMachine.OpenSubKey("Software\\Microsoft\\Windows NT\\CurrentVersion").GetValueNames();

            FileSystemObject fso = new FileSystemObject();
            TextStream txtstream =
fso.OpenTextFile(System.Environment.CurrentDirectory +
"\\OSInfo.html", IOMode.ForWriting, true,
Tristate.TristateUseDefault);
            txtstream.WriteLine("<hmtl>");
            txtstream.WriteLine("<head>");
            txtstream.WriteLine("<title></title>");
```

```
txtstream.WriteLine("<style type=text/css>");
txtstream.WriteLine("#itsthetable {");
txtstream.WriteLine("  font-family: Georgia, \"Times
New Roman\", Times, serif;");
txtstream.WriteLine("  color: #036;");
txtstream.WriteLine("}");

txtstream.WriteLine("caption {");
txtstream.WriteLine("  font-size: 48px;");
txtstream.WriteLine("  color: #036;");
txtstream.WriteLine("  font-weight: bolder;");
txtstream.WriteLine("  font-variant: small-caps;");
txtstream.WriteLine("}");

txtstream.WriteLine("th {");
txtstream.WriteLine("  font-size: 12px;");
txtstream.WriteLine("  color: #FFF;");
txtstream.WriteLine("  background-color: #06C;");
txtstream.WriteLine("  padding: 8px 4px;");
txtstream.WriteLine("  border-bottom: 1px solid
#015ebc;");
txtstream.WriteLine("}");

txtstream.WriteLine("table {");
txtstream.WriteLine("  margin: 0;");
txtstream.WriteLine("  padding: 0;");
txtstream.WriteLine("  border-collapse: collapse;");
txtstream.WriteLine("  border: 1px solid #06C;");
txtstream.WriteLine("  width: 100%");
txtstream.WriteLine("}");

txtstream.WriteLine("#itsthetable th a:link,
#itsthetable th a:visited {");
txtstream.WriteLine("  color: #FFF;");
txtstream.WriteLine("  text-decoration: none;");
txtstream.WriteLine("  border-left: 5px solid #FFF;");
txtstream.WriteLine("  padding-left: 3px;");
txtstream.WriteLine("}");

txtstream.WriteLine("th a:hover, #itsthetable th
a:active {");
txtstream.WriteLine("  color: #F90;");
txtstream.WriteLine("  text-decoration: line-
through;");
txtstream.WriteLine("  border-left: 5px solid #F90;");
```

```
txtstream.WriteLine(" padding-left: 3px;");
txtstream.WriteLine("}");

txtstream.WriteLine("tbody th:hover {");
txtstream.WriteLine(" background-image:
url(imgs/tbody_hover.gif);");
txtstream.WriteLine(" background-position: bottom;");
txtstream.WriteLine(" background-repeat: repeat-x;");
txtstream.WriteLine("}");

txtstream.WriteLine("td {");
txtstream.WriteLine(" background-color: #f2f2f2;");
txtstream.WriteLine(" padding: 4px;");
txtstream.WriteLine(" font-size: 12px;");
txtstream.WriteLine("}");

txtstream.WriteLine("#itsthetable td:hover {");
txtstream.WriteLine(" background-color: #f8f8f8;");

txtstream.WriteLine("}");

txtstream.WriteLine("#itsthetable td a:link,
#itsthetable td a:visited {");
txtstream.WriteLine(" color: #039;");
txtstream.WriteLine(" text-decoration: none;");
txtstream.WriteLine(" border-left: 3px solid #039;");
txtstream.WriteLine(" padding-left: 3px;");
txtstream.WriteLine("}");

txtstream.WriteLine("#itsthetable td a:hover,
#itsthetable td a:active {");
txtstream.WriteLine(" color: #06C;");
txtstream.WriteLine(" text-decoration: line-
through;");
txtstream.WriteLine(" border-left: 3px solid #06C;");
txtstream.WriteLine(" padding-left: 3px;");
txtstream.WriteLine("}");

txtstream.WriteLine("#itsthetable th {");
txtstream.WriteLine(" text-align: left;");
txtstream.WriteLine(" width: 150px;");
txtstream.WriteLine("}");

txtstream.WriteLine("#itsthetable tr {");
```

```
        txtstream.WriteLine(" border-bottom: 1px solid
#CCC;");
        txtstream.WriteLine("}");

        txtstream.WriteLine("#itsthetable thead th {");
        txtstream.WriteLine(" background-image:
url(imgs/thead_back.gif);");
        txtstream.WriteLine(" background-repeat: repeat-x;");
        txtstream.WriteLine(" background-color: #06C;");
        txtstream.WriteLine(" height: 30px;");
        txtstream.WriteLine(" font-size: 18px;");
        txtstream.WriteLine(" text-align: center;");
        txtstream.WriteLine(" text-shadow: #333 2px 2px;");
        txtstream.WriteLine(" border: 2px;");
        txtstream.WriteLine("}");

        txtstream.WriteLine("#itsthetable tfoot th {");
        txtstream.WriteLine(" background-image:
url(imgs/tfoot_back.gif);");
        txtstream.WriteLine(" background-repeat: repeat-x;");
        txtstream.WriteLine(" background-color: #036;");
        txtstream.WriteLine(" height: 30px;");
        txtstream.WriteLine(" font-size: 28px;");
        txtstream.WriteLine(" text-align: center;");
        txtstream.WriteLine(" text-shadow: #333 2px 2px;");
        txtstream.WriteLine("}");

        txtstream.WriteLine("#itsthetable tfoot td {");
        txtstream.WriteLine(" background-image:
url(imgs/tfoot_back.gif);");
        txtstream.WriteLine(" background-repeat: repeat-x;");
        txtstream.WriteLine(" background-color: #036;");
        txtstream.WriteLine(" color: FFF;");
        txtstream.WriteLine(" height: 30px;");
        txtstream.WriteLine(" font-size: 24px;");
        txtstream.WriteLine(" text-align: left;");
        txtstream.WriteLine(" text-shadow: #333 2px 2px;");
        txtstream.WriteLine("}");

        txtstream.WriteLine("tbody td
a[href=\"http://www.csslab.cl/\"] {");
        txtstream.WriteLine(" font-weight: bolder;");
        txtstream.WriteLine("}");
        txtstream.WriteLine("</style>");
        txtstream.WriteLine("<body>");
```

```
            txtstream.WriteLine("<center>");
            txtstream.WriteLine("<table Style=\"Border:0;\">");
            txtstream.WriteLine("<tr><TH Nowrap
STYLE=\"background-color:white;FONT-WEIGHT:normal; FONT-SIZE:
48px; COLOR: navy; FONT-STYLE: normal; FONT-FAMILY: Edwardian
Script ITC\"></TH></tr>");
            txtstream.WriteLine("</table>");
            txtstream.WriteLine("<table
style=\"border:Double;border-width:1px;border-color:navy;\"
cellpadding=2 cellspacing=2 Width=0>");
            txtstream.WriteLine("<tr>");
            txtstream.WriteLine("    <th align=\"left\">Value
Name</th>");
            txtstream.WriteLine("    <th align=\"left\">Reg
Type</th>");
            txtstream.WriteLine("    <th
align=\"left\">Value</th>");
            txtstream.WriteLine("</tr>");

            string name = "";
            string nk = "";
            string value = "";


            foreach (string v in names)
            {
                object vv =
Registry.LocalMachine.OpenSubKey("Software\\Microsoft\\Windows
NT\\CurrentVersion").GetValue(v);
                RegistryValueKind vk =
Registry.LocalMachine.OpenSubKey("Software\\Microsoft\\Windows
NT\\CurrentVersion").GetValueKind(v);
                switch (vk)
                {
                    case RegistryValueKind.String:
                        {
                            name = v;
                            nk = "REG_SZ";
                            value = vv.ToString();
                            break;
                        }
                    case RegistryValueKind.ExpandString:
                        {
                            name = v;
                            nk = "REG_Expand_SZ";
```

```csharp
                                 value = vv.ToString();
                                 break;
                         }
                    case RegistryValueKind.MultiString:
                         {
                             name = v;
                             nk = "REG_MULTI_SZ";
                             string[] mchammer = (string[])vv;
                             value = "";
                             for (int i = 0; i <
mchammer.GetLength(0); i++)
                             {
                                 if (value != "")
                                 {
                                     value = value + ", ";
                                 }
                                 value = value +
mchammer.GetValue(i).ToString();
                             }
                             break;
                         }
                    case RegistryValueKind.DWord:
                         {
                             name = v;
                             nk = "REG_DWORD";
                             int l = (int)vv;
                             value = "(0x" + l.ToString("X8") + ")
" + l.ToString();
                             break;
                         }
                    case RegistryValueKind.QWord:
                         {
                             name = v;
                             nk = "REG_QWORD";
                             int l = (int)vv;
                             value = "(0x" + l.ToString("X8") + ")
" + l.ToString();
                             break;
                         }
                    case RegistryValueKind.Binary:
                         {
                             byte[] bi = (byte[])vv;
                             name = v;
                             nk = "REG_BINARY";
                             string tempstr = "";
```

```csharp
                    int len = bi.Length;
                    for (int i = 0; i < len; i++)
                    {
                        tempstr = bi[i].ToString("x");
                        if (tempstr.Length == 1)
                        {
                            tempstr = "0" + tempstr;
                        }
                        value = value + tempstr + " ";
                        tempstr = "";
                    }
                    break;
                }

            }
            if (v == "")
            {
                name = "(Default)";
            }
            txtstream.WriteLine("<tr>");
            txtstream.WriteLine("    <td align=\"left\">" +
name + "</td>");
            txtstream.WriteLine("    <td align=\"left\">" +
nk + "</td>");
            txtstream.WriteLine("    <td align=\"left\">" +
value + "</td>");
            txtstream.WriteLine("</tr>");

        }
        txtstream.WriteLine("</table>");
        txtstream.WriteLine("</body>");
        txtstream.WriteLine("</html>");
        txtstream.Close();


webBrowser1.Navigate(System.Environment.CurrentDirectory +
"\\OSInfo.html");
        }

    }
}
```

Here's what the output looks like.

Value Name	Reg Type	Value
BaseBuildRevisionNumber	REG_DWORD	(0x00000001) 1
BuildBranch	REG_SZ	19h1_release
BuildGUID	REG_SZ	ffffffff-ffff-ffff-ffff-ffffffffffff
BuildLab	REG_SZ	18362.19h1_release.190318-1202
BuildLabEx	REG_SZ	18362.1.amd64fre.19h1_release.190318-1202
CompositionEditionID	REG_SZ	Enterprise
CurrentBuild	REG_SZ	18363
CurrentBuildNumber	REG_SZ	18363
CurrentMajorVersionNumber	REG_DWORD	(0x0000000A) 10
CurrentMinorVersionNumber	REG_DWORD	(0x00000000) 0
CurrentType	REG_SZ	Multiprocessor Free
CurrentVersion	REG_SZ	6.3
EditionID	REG_SZ	Enterprise
EditionSubManufacturer	REG_SZ	
EditionSubstring	REG_SZ	
EditionSubVersion	REG_SZ	
InstallationType	REG_SZ	Client
InstallDate	REG_DWORD	(0x00000000) 0
ProductName	REG_SZ	Windows 10 Enterprise
ReleaseId	REG_SZ	1909
SoftwareType	REG_SZ	System
SystemRoot	REG_SZ	C:\Windows
UBR	REG_DWORD	(0x00000217) 535
RegisteredOwner	REG_SZ	REDWAR2009@hotmail.com
RegisteredOrganization	REG_SZ	
PathName	REG_SZ	C:\Windows

What about Session Information?

Isn't that where PendingfileRenamingOperations exists?

```
using System;
using System.Collections.Generic;
using System.Linq;
using System.Text;
using Microsoft.Win32;
using Scripting;
namespace ListRegistryEntries
{
    class ClsOSInformation
    {
        public void Get_OS_Info(System.Windows.Forms.WebBrowser
webBrowser1)
        {
            System.Collections.Generic.Dictionary<string, string>
pidy = new System.Collections.Generic.Dictionary<string,
string>();
            String[] names =
Registry.LocalMachine.OpenSubKey("SYSTEM\\CurrentControlSet\\Cont
rol\\Session Manager").GetValueNames();
```

```csharp
            FileSystemObject fso = new FileSystemObject();
            TextStream txtstream =
fso.OpenTextFile(System.Environment.CurrentDirectory +
"\\Session.html", IOMode.ForWriting, true,
Tristate.TristateUseDefault);
            txtstream.WriteLine("<hmtl>");
            txtstream.WriteLine("<head>");
            txtstream.WriteLine("<title></title>");
            txtstream.WriteLine("<style type=text/css>");
            txtstream.WriteLine("#itsthetable {");
            txtstream.WriteLine(" font-family: Georgia, \"Times
New Roman\", Times, serif;");
            txtstream.WriteLine(" color: #036;");
            txtstream.WriteLine("}");

            txtstream.WriteLine("caption {");
            txtstream.WriteLine(" font-size: 48px;");
            txtstream.WriteLine(" color: #036;");
            txtstream.WriteLine(" font-weight: bolder;");
            txtstream.WriteLine(" font-variant: small-caps;");
            txtstream.WriteLine("}");

            txtstream.WriteLine("th {");
            txtstream.WriteLine(" font-size: 12px;");
            txtstream.WriteLine(" color: #FFF;");
            txtstream.WriteLine(" background-color: #06C;");
            txtstream.WriteLine(" padding: 8px 4px;");
            txtstream.WriteLine(" border-bottom: 1px solid
#015ebc;");
            txtstream.WriteLine("}");

            txtstream.WriteLine("table {");
            txtstream.WriteLine(" margin: 0;");
            txtstream.WriteLine(" padding: 0;");
            txtstream.WriteLine(" border-collapse: collapse;");
            txtstream.WriteLine(" border: 1px solid #06C;");
            txtstream.WriteLine(" width: 100%");
            txtstream.WriteLine("}");

            txtstream.WriteLine("#itsthetable th a:link,
#itsthetable th a:visited {");
            txtstream.WriteLine(" color: #FFF;");
            txtstream.WriteLine(" text-decoration: none;");
            txtstream.WriteLine(" border-left: 5px solid #FFF;");
            txtstream.WriteLine(" padding-left: 3px;");
```

```
txtstream.WriteLine("}");

txtstream.WriteLine("th a:hover, #itsthetable th
a:active {");
txtstream.WriteLine("  color: #F90;");
txtstream.WriteLine("  text-decoration: line-
through;");
txtstream.WriteLine("  border-left: 5px solid #F90;");
txtstream.WriteLine("  padding-left: 3px;");
txtstream.WriteLine("}");

txtstream.WriteLine("tbody th:hover {");
txtstream.WriteLine("  background-image:
url(imgs/tbody_hover.gif);");
txtstream.WriteLine("  background-position: bottom;");
txtstream.WriteLine("  background-repeat: repeat-x;");
txtstream.WriteLine("}");

txtstream.WriteLine("td {");
txtstream.WriteLine("  background-color: #f2f2f2;");
txtstream.WriteLine("  padding: 4px;");
txtstream.WriteLine("  font-size: 12px;");
txtstream.WriteLine("}");

txtstream.WriteLine("#itsthetable td:hover {");
txtstream.WriteLine("  background-color: #f8f8f8;");

txtstream.WriteLine("}");

txtstream.WriteLine("#itsthetable td a:link,
#itsthetable td a:visited {");
txtstream.WriteLine("  color: #039;");
txtstream.WriteLine("  text-decoration: none;");
txtstream.WriteLine("  border-left: 3px solid #039;");
txtstream.WriteLine("  padding-left: 3px;");
txtstream.WriteLine("}");

txtstream.WriteLine("#itsthetable td a:hover,
#itsthetable td a:active {");
txtstream.WriteLine("  color: #06C;");
txtstream.WriteLine("  text-decoration: line-
through;");
txtstream.WriteLine("  border-left: 3px solid #06C;");
txtstream.WriteLine("  padding-left: 3px;");
txtstream.WriteLine("}");
```

```
txtstream.WriteLine("#itsthetable th {");
txtstream.WriteLine(" text-align: left;");
txtstream.WriteLine(" width: 150px;");
txtstream.WriteLine("}");

txtstream.WriteLine("#itsthetable tr {");
txtstream.WriteLine(" border-bottom: 1px solid
#CCC;");
txtstream.WriteLine("}");

txtstream.WriteLine("#itsthetable thead th {");
txtstream.WriteLine(" background-image:
url(imgs/thead_back.gif);");
txtstream.WriteLine(" background-repeat: repeat-x;");
txtstream.WriteLine(" background-color: #06C;");
txtstream.WriteLine(" height: 30px;");
txtstream.WriteLine(" font-size: 18px;");
txtstream.WriteLine(" text-align: center;");
txtstream.WriteLine(" text-shadow: #333 2px 2px;");
txtstream.WriteLine(" border: 2px;");
txtstream.WriteLine("}");

txtstream.WriteLine("#itsthetable tfoot th {");
txtstream.WriteLine(" background-image:
url(imgs/tfoot_back.gif);");
txtstream.WriteLine(" background-repeat: repeat-x;");
txtstream.WriteLine(" background-color: #036;");
txtstream.WriteLine(" height: 30px;");
txtstream.WriteLine(" font-size: 28px;");
txtstream.WriteLine(" text-align: center;");
txtstream.WriteLine(" text-shadow: #333 2px 2px;");
txtstream.WriteLine("}");

txtstream.WriteLine("#itsthetable tfoot td {");
txtstream.WriteLine(" background-image:
url(imgs/tfoot_back.gif);");
txtstream.WriteLine(" background-repeat: repeat-x;");
txtstream.WriteLine(" background-color: #036;");
txtstream.WriteLine(" color: FFF;");
txtstream.WriteLine(" height: 30px;");
txtstream.WriteLine(" font-size: 24px;");
txtstream.WriteLine(" text-align: left;");
txtstream.WriteLine(" text-shadow: #333 2px 2px;");
txtstream.WriteLine("}");
```

```
            txtstream.WriteLine("tbody td
a[href=\"http://www.csslab.cl/\"] {");
            txtstream.WriteLine("  font-weight: bolder;");
            txtstream.WriteLine("}");
            txtstream.WriteLine("</style>");
            txtstream.WriteLine("<body>");
            txtstream.WriteLine("<center>");
            txtstream.WriteLine("<table Style=\"Border:0;\">");
            txtstream.WriteLine("<tr><TH Nowrap
STYLE=\"background-color:white;FONT-WEIGHT:normal; FONT-SIZE:
48px; COLOR: navy; FONT-STYLE: normal; FONT-FAMILY: Edwardian
Script ITC\"></TH></tr>");
            txtstream.WriteLine("</table>");
            txtstream.WriteLine("<table
style=\"border:Double;border-width:1px;border-color:navy;\"
cellpadding=2 cellspacing=2 Width=0>");
            txtstream.WriteLine("<tr>");
            txtstream.WriteLine("    <th align=\"left\">Value
Name</th>");
            txtstream.WriteLine("    <th align=\"left\">Reg
Type</th>");
            txtstream.WriteLine("    <th
align=\"left\">Value</th>");
            txtstream.WriteLine("</tr>");

            string name = "";
            string nk = "";
            string value = "";


            foreach (string v in names)
            {
                object vv =
Registry.LocalMachine.OpenSubKey("SYSTEM\\CurrentControlSet\\Cont
rol\\Session Manager").GetValue(v);
                RegistryValueKind vk =
Registry.LocalMachine.OpenSubKey("SYSTEM\\CurrentControlSet\\Cont
rol\\Session Manager").GetValueKind(v);
                switch (vk)
                {
                    case RegistryValueKind.String:
                        {
                            name = v;
                            nk = "REG_SZ";
```

```csharp
                        value = vv.ToString();
                        break;
                    }
                case RegistryValueKind.ExpandString:
                    {
                        name = v;
                        nk = "REG_Expand_SZ";
                        value = vv.ToString();
                        break;
                    }
                case RegistryValueKind.MultiString:
                    {
                        name = v;
                        nk = "REG_MULTI_SZ";
                        string[] mchammer = (string[])vv;
                        value = "";
                        for (int i = 0; i <
mchammer.GetLength(0); i++)
                        {
                            if (value != "")
                            {
                                value = value + ", ";
                            }
                            value = value +
mchammer.GetValue(i).ToString();
                        }
                        break;
                    }
                case RegistryValueKind.DWord:
                    {
                        name = v;
                        nk = "REG_DWORD";
                        int l = (int)vv;
                        value = "(0x" + l.ToString("X8") + ")
" + l.ToString();
                        break;
                    }
                case RegistryValueKind.QWord:
                    {
                        name = v;
                        nk = "REG_QWORD";
                        int l = (int)vv;
                        value = "(0x" + l.ToString("X8") + ")
" + l.ToString();
                        break;
```

```csharp
                        }
                case RegistryValueKind.Binary:
                    {
                        byte[] bi = (byte[])vv;
                        name = v;
                        nk = "REG_BINARY";
                        string tempstr = "";
                        int len = bi.Length;
                        for (int i = 0; i < len; i++)
                        {
                            tempstr = bi[i].ToString("x");
                            if (tempstr.Length == 1)
                            {
                                tempstr = "0" + tempstr;
                            }
                            value = value + tempstr + " ";
                            tempstr = "";
                        }
                        break;
                    }

                }
                if (v == "")
                {
                    name = "(Default)";
                }
                txtstream.WriteLine("<tr>");
                txtstream.WriteLine("    <td align=\"left\">" +
name + "</td>");
                txtstream.WriteLine("    <td align=\"left\">" +
nk + "</td>");
                txtstream.WriteLine("    <td align=\"left\">" +
value + "</td>");
                txtstream.WriteLine("</tr>");

            }
            txtstream.WriteLine("</table>");
            txtstream.WriteLine("</body>");
            txtstream.WriteLine("</html>");
            txtstream.Close();


webBrowser1.Navigate(System.Environment.CurrentDirectory +
"\\Session.html");
        }
```

```
        }
}
```

Well, I guess it does!

Value Name	Reg Type	Value
AutoChkTimeout	REG_DWORD	(0x0000000) 1
BootExecute	REG_MULTI_SZ	autocheck autochk *
BootShell	REG_Expand_SZ	C:\Windows\system32\Boot.exe
CriticalSectionTimeout	REG_DWORD	(0x0278D00) 2592000
ExcludeFromKnownDlls	REG_MULTI_SZ	
GlobalFlag	REG_DWORD	(0x0000000) 0
GlobalFlag2	REG_DWORD	(0x0000000) 0
HeapDeCommitFreeBlockThreshold	REG_DWORD	(0x0000000) 0
HeapDeCommitTotalFreeThreshold	REG_DWORD	(0x0000000) 0
HeapSegmentCommit	REG_DWORD	(0x0000000) 0
HeapSegmentReserve	REG_DWORD	(0x0000000) 0
InitConsoleFlags	REG_DWORD	(0x0000000) 0
NumberOfInitialSessions	REG_DWORD	(0x0000002) 2
ObjectDirectories	REG_MULTI_SZ	Windows\ RPC Control
ProcessorControl	REG_DWORD	(0x0000002) 2
ProtectionMode	REG_DWORD	(0x0000001) 1
ResourceTimeoutCount	REG_DWORD	(0x0000096) 150
RunLevelExecute	REG_MULTI_SZ	Winlstr, ServiceControlManager
RunLevelValidate	REG_MULTI_SZ	ServiceControlManager
SETUPEXECUTE	REG_MULTI_SZ	
AutoChkSkipSystemPartition	REG_DWORD	(0x0000000) 0
PendingFileRenameOperation	REG_MULTI_SZ	"?\C:\Windows\system32\spool\V4Drv\E652826A-1F12-49DB-B3B3-98C2BB1\E0847f6af2.BUD., "?\C:\Windows\system32\spool\V4Drv\E652826A-1F12-49DB-B3B2-98C2BB1820, "?\C:\Windows\system32\spool\V4Drv\E652826A-1F12-49DB-B3B2-98C2BB1820, \847:86af2.gpd., "?\C:\Windows\system32\spool\V4Drv\E652826A-1F12-49DB-B3B3-98C2BB1820.

What if I just wanted to know if that specific value existed?

```
using System;
using System.Collections.Generic;
using System.ComponentModel;
using System.Data;
using System.Drawing;
using System.Linq;
using System.Text;
using System.Windows.Forms;
using Microsoft.Win32;
using Scripting;

namespace Pending
{
    public partial class Form1 : Form
    {
        public Form1()
        {
            InitializeComponent();
        }

        private void Form1_Load(object sender, EventArgs e)
        {
```

```csharp
            RegistryKey regkey =
Registry.LocalMachine.OpenSubKey("SYSTEM\\CurrentControlSet\\Cont
rol\\Session Manager");
            try
            {
                Object value =
(Object)regkey.GetValue("PendingFileRenameOperations");
                Generate_Report();

            }
            catch(Exception ex)
            {

            }

        }
        public void Generate_Report()
        {
            System.Collections.Generic.Dictionary<string, string>
pidy = new System.Collections.Generic.Dictionary<string,
string>();

            FileSystemObject fso = new FileSystemObject();
            TextStream txtstream =
fso.OpenTextFile(System.Environment.CurrentDirectory +
"\\Pending.html", IOMode.ForWriting, true,
Tristate.TristateUseDefault);
            txtstream.WriteLine("<hmtl>");
            txtstream.WriteLine("<head>");
            txtstream.WriteLine("<title></title>");
            txtstream.WriteLine("<style type=text/css>");
            txtstream.WriteLine("#itsthetable {");
            txtstream.WriteLine(" font-family: Georgia, \"Times
New Roman\", Times, serif;");
            txtstream.WriteLine(" color: #036;");
            txtstream.WriteLine("}");

            txtstream.WriteLine("caption {");
            txtstream.WriteLine(" font-size: 48px;");
            txtstream.WriteLine(" color: #036;");
            txtstream.WriteLine(" font-weight: bolder;");
            txtstream.WriteLine(" font-variant: small-caps;");
            txtstream.WriteLine("}");

            txtstream.WriteLine("th {");
```

```
txtstream.WriteLine(" font-size: 12px;");
txtstream.WriteLine(" color: #FFF;");
txtstream.WriteLine(" background-color: #06C;");
txtstream.WriteLine(" padding: 8px 4px;");
txtstream.WriteLine(" border-bottom: 1px solid
#015ebc;");
txtstream.WriteLine("}");

txtstream.WriteLine("table {");
txtstream.WriteLine(" margin: 0;");
txtstream.WriteLine(" padding: 0;");
txtstream.WriteLine(" border-collapse: collapse;");
txtstream.WriteLine(" border: 1px solid #06C;");
txtstream.WriteLine(" width: 100%");
txtstream.WriteLine("}");

txtstream.WriteLine("#itsthetable th a:link,
#itsthetable th a:visited {");
txtstream.WriteLine(" color: #FFF;");
txtstream.WriteLine(" text-decoration: none;");
txtstream.WriteLine(" border-left: 5px solid #FFF;");
txtstream.WriteLine(" padding-left: 3px;");
txtstream.WriteLine("}");

txtstream.WriteLine("th a:hover, #itsthetable th
a:active {");
txtstream.WriteLine(" color: #F90;");
txtstream.WriteLine(" text-decoration: line-
through;");
txtstream.WriteLine(" border-left: 5px solid #F90;");
txtstream.WriteLine(" padding-left: 3px;");
txtstream.WriteLine("}");

txtstream.WriteLine("tbody th:hover {");
txtstream.WriteLine(" background-image:
url(imgs/tbody_hover.gif);");
txtstream.WriteLine(" background-position: bottom;");
txtstream.WriteLine(" background-repeat: repeat-x;");
txtstream.WriteLine("}");

txtstream.WriteLine("td {");
txtstream.WriteLine(" background-color: #f2f2f2;");
txtstream.WriteLine(" padding: 4px;");
txtstream.WriteLine(" font-size: 12px;");
txtstream.WriteLine("}");
```

```
            txtstream.WriteLine("#itsthetable td:hover {");
            txtstream.WriteLine(" background-color: #f8f8f8;");

            txtstream.WriteLine("}");

            txtstream.WriteLine("#itsthetable td a:link,
    #itsthetable td a:visited {");
            txtstream.WriteLine(" color: #039;");
            txtstream.WriteLine(" text-decoration: none;");
            txtstream.WriteLine(" border-left: 3px solid #039;");
            txtstream.WriteLine(" padding-left: 3px;");
            txtstream.WriteLine("}");

            txtstream.WriteLine("#itsthetable td a:hover,
    #itsthetable td a:active {");
            txtstream.WriteLine(" color: #06C;");
            txtstream.WriteLine(" text-decoration: line-
    through;");
            txtstream.WriteLine(" border-left: 3px solid #06C;");
            txtstream.WriteLine(" padding-left: 3px;");
            txtstream.WriteLine("}");

            txtstream.WriteLine("#itsthetable th {");
            txtstream.WriteLine(" text-align: left;");
            txtstream.WriteLine(" width: 150px;");
            txtstream.WriteLine("}");

            txtstream.WriteLine("#itsthetable tr {");
            txtstream.WriteLine(" border-bottom: 1px solid
    #CCC;");
            txtstream.WriteLine("}");

            txtstream.WriteLine("#itsthetable thead th {");
            txtstream.WriteLine(" background-image:
    url(imgs/thead_back.gif);");
            txtstream.WriteLine(" background-repeat: repeat-x;");
            txtstream.WriteLine(" background-color: #06C;");
            txtstream.WriteLine(" height: 30px;");
            txtstream.WriteLine(" font-size: 18px;");
            txtstream.WriteLine(" text-align: center;");
            txtstream.WriteLine(" text-shadow: #333 2px 2px;");
            txtstream.WriteLine(" border: 2px;");
            txtstream.WriteLine("}");
```

```
        txtstream.WriteLine("#itsthetable tfoot th {");
        txtstream.WriteLine("  background-image:
url(imgs/tfoot_back.gif);");
        txtstream.WriteLine("  background-repeat: repeat-x;");
        txtstream.WriteLine("  background-color: #036;");
        txtstream.WriteLine("  height: 30px;");
        txtstream.WriteLine("  font-size: 28px;");
        txtstream.WriteLine("  text-align: center;");
        txtstream.WriteLine("  text-shadow: #333 2px 2px;");
        txtstream.WriteLine("}");

        txtstream.WriteLine("#itsthetable tfoot td {");
        txtstream.WriteLine("  background-image:
url(imgs/tfoot_back.gif);");
        txtstream.WriteLine("  background-repeat: repeat-x;");
        txtstream.WriteLine("  background-color: #036;");
        txtstream.WriteLine("  color: FFF;");
        txtstream.WriteLine("  height: 30px;");
        txtstream.WriteLine("  font-size: 24px;");
        txtstream.WriteLine("  text-align: left;");
        txtstream.WriteLine("  text-shadow: #333 2px 2px;");
        txtstream.WriteLine("}");

        txtstream.WriteLine("tbody td
a[href=\"http://www.csslab.cl/\"] {");
        txtstream.WriteLine("  font-weight: bolder;");
        txtstream.WriteLine("}");
        txtstream.WriteLine("</style>");
        txtstream.WriteLine("<body>");
        txtstream.WriteLine("<center>");
        txtstream.WriteLine("<table Style=\"Border:0;\">");
        txtstream.WriteLine("<tr><TH Nowrap
STYLE=\"background-color:white;FONT-WEIGHT:normal; FONT-SIZE:
48px; COLOR: navy; FONT-STYLE: normal; FONT-FAMILY: Edwardian
Script ITC\"></TH></tr>");
        txtstream.WriteLine("</table>");
        txtstream.WriteLine("<table
style=\"border:Double;border-width:1px;border-color:navy;\"
cellpadding=2 cellspacing=2 Width=0>");
        txtstream.WriteLine("<tr>");
        txtstream.WriteLine("    <th align=\"left\">Value
Name</th>");
        txtstream.WriteLine("    <th align=\"left\">Reg
Type</th>");
```

```csharp
            txtstream.WriteLine("    <th
align=\"left\">Value</th>");
            txtstream.WriteLine("</tr>");

            string name = "";
            string nk = "";
            string value = "";


                object vv =
Registry.LocalMachine.OpenSubKey("SYSTEM\\CurrentControlSet\\Cont
rol\\Session Manager").GetValue("PendingFileRenameOperations");
            name = "PendingFileRenameOperations";
            nk = "REG_MULTI_SZ";
            string[] mchammer = (string[])vv;
            value = "";
            for (int i = 0; i < mchammer.GetLength(0); i++)
            {
                if (value != "")
                {
                    value = value + ", ";
                }
                value = value +
mchammer.GetValue(i).ToString();
            }

            txtstream.WriteLine("<tr>");
            txtstream.WriteLine("    <td align=\"left\">" + name
+ "</td>");
            txtstream.WriteLine("    <td align=\"left\">" + nk +
"</td>");
            txtstream.WriteLine("    <td align=\"left\">" + value
+ "</td>");
            txtstream.WriteLine("</tr>");
            txtstream.WriteLine("</table>");
            txtstream.WriteLine("</body>");
            txtstream.WriteLine("</html>");
            txtstream.Close();


webBrowser1.Navigate(System.Environment.CurrentDirectory +
"\\Pending.html");
        }

    }
```

```
}
```

The code will either show nothing or report that it exists and display the values:

Value Name	Reg Type	Value
PendingFileRenameOperations	REG_MULTI_SZ	\??\C:\Windows\system32\spool\V4Dirs\E652826A-1F12-49DB-B3B2-9890E2BB1820\94766af2.BUD, , \??\C:\Windows\system32\spool\V4Dirs\E652826A-1F12-49DB-B3B2-9890E2BB1820\94766af2.gpd, , \??\C:\Windows\system32\spool\V4Dirs\E652826A-1F12-49DB-B3B2-9890E2BB1820,

Isn't there a there a section in the registry that details installed products? In HKEY_CLASSES_ROOT, there is a subkey named "Installer". This particular registry key exposes the following subkeys:

1. Assemblies
2. Components
3. Dependencies
4. Features
5. Patches
6. Products
7. UpgradeCodes
8. Win32Assemblies

Because this is such an important section of the registry, I created a program specifically designed to read and view its content:

```
using System;
using System.Collections.Generic;
using System.ComponentModel;
using System.Data;
using System.Drawing;
using System.Linq;
using System.Text;
using System.Windows.Forms;
using Microsoft.Win32;
using Scripting;
```

```csharp
namespace ListRegistryEntries
{
    public partial class Form1 : Form
    {
        public Form1()
        {
            InitializeComponent();
        }

        private void Form1_Load(object sender, EventArgs e)
        {
            comboBox1.Text = "*Select a Subkey*";
            comboBox1.Items.Add("*Select a Subkey*");
            string[] names =
Registry.ClassesRoot.OpenSubKey("Installer").GetSubKeyNames();
            foreach (string n in names)
            {
                comboBox1.Items.Add(n);
            }
        }

        private void comboBox1_SelectedIndexChanged(object
sender, EventArgs e)
        {
            if (comboBox1.Text != "*Select a Subkey*")
            {
                treeView1.Nodes.Clear();
                string[] names =
Registry.ClassesRoot.OpenSubKey("Installer\\" +
comboBox1.Text).GetSubKeyNames();
                foreach (string n in names)
                {
                    treeView1.Nodes.Add(n);
                }
            }
        }

        private void treeView1_AfterSelect(object sender,
TreeViewEventArgs e)
        {
            if (treeView1.SelectedNode.Nodes.Count == 0)
            {
```

```csharp
                string[] names =
Registry.ClassesRoot.OpenSubKey("Installer\\" + comboBox1.Text +
"\\" + treeView1.SelectedNode.FullPath).GetSubKeyNames();
                foreach (string n in names)
                {
                    treeView1.SelectedNode.Nodes.Add(n);
                }
                Get_Values("Installer\\" + comboBox1.Text + "\\"
+ treeView1.SelectedNode.FullPath);
            }
            else
            {
                Get_Values("Installer\\" + comboBox1.Text + "\\"
+ treeView1.SelectedNode.FullPath);
            }
        }
        public void Get_Values(string path)
        {
            System.Collections.Generic.Dictionary<string, string>
pidy = new System.Collections.Generic.Dictionary<string,
string>();
            String[] names =
Registry.ClassesRoot.OpenSubKey(path).GetValueNames();

            FileSystemObject fso = new FileSystemObject();
            TextStream txtstream =
fso.OpenTextFile(System.Environment.CurrentDirectory + "\\" +
comboBox1.Text + ".html", IOMode.ForWriting, true,
Tristate.TristateUseDefault);
            txtstream.WriteLine("<hmtl>");
            txtstream.WriteLine("<head>");
            txtstream.WriteLine("<title></title>");
            txtstream.WriteLine("<style type=text/css>");
            txtstream.WriteLine("#itsthetable {");
            txtstream.WriteLine(" font-family: Georgia, \"Times
New Roman\", Times, serif;");
            txtstream.WriteLine(" color: #036;");
            txtstream.WriteLine("}");

            txtstream.WriteLine("caption {");
            txtstream.WriteLine(" font-size: 48px;");
            txtstream.WriteLine(" color: #036;");
            txtstream.WriteLine(" font-weight: bolder;");
            txtstream.WriteLine(" font-variant: small-caps;");
            txtstream.WriteLine("}");
```

```
            txtstream.WriteLine("th {");
            txtstream.WriteLine("  font-size: 12px;");
            txtstream.WriteLine("  color: #FFF;");
            txtstream.WriteLine("  background-color: #06C;");
            txtstream.WriteLine("  padding: 8px 4px;");
            txtstream.WriteLine("  border-bottom: 1px solid
#015ebc;");
            txtstream.WriteLine("}");

            txtstream.WriteLine("table {");
            txtstream.WriteLine("  margin: 0;");
            txtstream.WriteLine("  padding: 0;");
            txtstream.WriteLine("  border-collapse: collapse;");
            txtstream.WriteLine("  border: 1px solid #06C;");
            txtstream.WriteLine("  width: 100%");
            txtstream.WriteLine("}");

            txtstream.WriteLine("#itsthetable th a:link,
#itsthetable th a:visited {");
            txtstream.WriteLine("  color: #FFF;");
            txtstream.WriteLine("  text-decoration: none;");
            txtstream.WriteLine("  border-left: 5px solid #FFF;");
            txtstream.WriteLine("  padding-left: 3px;");
            txtstream.WriteLine("}");

            txtstream.WriteLine("th a:hover, #itsthetable th
a:active {");
            txtstream.WriteLine("  color: #F90;");
            txtstream.WriteLine("  text-decoration: line-
through;");
            txtstream.WriteLine("  border-left: 5px solid #F90;");
            txtstream.WriteLine("  padding-left: 3px;");
            txtstream.WriteLine("}");

            txtstream.WriteLine("tbody th:hover {");
            txtstream.WriteLine("  background-image:
url(imgs/tbody_hover.gif);");
            txtstream.WriteLine("  background-position: bottom;");
            txtstream.WriteLine("  background-repeat: repeat-x;");
            txtstream.WriteLine("}");

            txtstream.WriteLine("td {");
            txtstream.WriteLine("  background-color: #f2f2f2;");
            txtstream.WriteLine("  padding: 4px;");
```

```
            txtstream.WriteLine("  font-size: 12px;");
            txtstream.WriteLine("}");

            txtstream.WriteLine("#itsthetable td:hover {");
            txtstream.WriteLine("  background-color: #f8f8f8;");

            txtstream.WriteLine("}");

            txtstream.WriteLine("#itsthetable td a:link,
#itsthetable td a:visited {");
            txtstream.WriteLine("  color: #039;");
            txtstream.WriteLine("  text-decoration: none;");
            txtstream.WriteLine("  border-left: 3px solid #039;");
            txtstream.WriteLine("  padding-left: 3px;");
            txtstream.WriteLine("}");

            txtstream.WriteLine("#itsthetable td a:hover,
#itsthetable td a:active {");
            txtstream.WriteLine("  color: #06C;");
            txtstream.WriteLine("  text-decoration: line-
through;");
            txtstream.WriteLine("  border-left: 3px solid #06C;");
            txtstream.WriteLine("  padding-left: 3px;");
            txtstream.WriteLine("}");

            txtstream.WriteLine("#itsthetable th {");
            txtstream.WriteLine("  text-align: left;");
            txtstream.WriteLine("  width: 150px;");
            txtstream.WriteLine("}");

            txtstream.WriteLine("#itsthetable tr {");
            txtstream.WriteLine("  border-bottom: 1px solid
#CCC;");
            txtstream.WriteLine("}");

            txtstream.WriteLine("#itsthetable thead th {");
            txtstream.WriteLine("  background-image:
url(imgs/thead_back.gif);");
            txtstream.WriteLine("  background-repeat: repeat-x;");
            txtstream.WriteLine("  background-color: #06C;");
            txtstream.WriteLine("  height: 30px;");
            txtstream.WriteLine("  font-size: 18px;");
            txtstream.WriteLine("  text-align: center;");
            txtstream.WriteLine("  text-shadow: #333 2px 2px;");
            txtstream.WriteLine("  border: 2px;");
```

```
            txtstream.WriteLine("}");

            txtstream.WriteLine("#itsthetable tfoot th {");
            txtstream.WriteLine(" background-image:
url(imgs/tfoot_back.gif);");
            txtstream.WriteLine(" background-repeat: repeat-x;");
            txtstream.WriteLine(" background-color: #036;");
            txtstream.WriteLine(" height: 30px;");
            txtstream.WriteLine(" font-size: 28px;");
            txtstream.WriteLine(" text-align: center;");
            txtstream.WriteLine(" text-shadow: #333 2px 2px;");
            txtstream.WriteLine("}");

            txtstream.WriteLine("#itsthetable tfoot td {");
            txtstream.WriteLine(" background-image:
url(imgs/tfoot_back.gif);");
            txtstream.WriteLine(" background-repeat: repeat-x;");
            txtstream.WriteLine(" background-color: #036;");
            txtstream.WriteLine(" color: FFF;");
            txtstream.WriteLine(" height: 30px;");
            txtstream.WriteLine(" font-size: 24px;");
            txtstream.WriteLine(" text-align: left;");
            txtstream.WriteLine(" text-shadow: #333 2px 2px;");
            txtstream.WriteLine("}");

            txtstream.WriteLine("tbody td
a[href=\"http://www.csslab.cl/\"] {");
            txtstream.WriteLine(" font-weight: bolder;");
            txtstream.WriteLine("}");
            txtstream.WriteLine("</style>");
            txtstream.WriteLine("<body>");
            txtstream.WriteLine("<center>");
            txtstream.WriteLine("<table Style=\"Border:0;\">");
            txtstream.WriteLine("<tr><TH Nowrap
STYLE=\"background-color:white;FONT-WEIGHT:normal; FONT-SIZE:
48px; COLOR: navy; FONT-STYLE: normal; FONT-FAMILY: Edwardian
Script ITC\"></TH></tr>");
            txtstream.WriteLine("</table>");
            txtstream.WriteLine("<table
style=\"border:Double;border-width:1px;border-color:navy;\"
cellpadding=2 cellspacing=2 Width=0>");
            txtstream.WriteLine("<tr>");
            txtstream.WriteLine("    <th align=\"left\">Value
Name</th>");
```

```csharp
            txtstream.WriteLine("     <th align=\"left\">Reg
Type</th>");
            txtstream.WriteLine("     <th
align=\"left\">Value</th>");
            txtstream.WriteLine("</tr>");

            string name = "";
            string nk = "";
            string value = "";


            foreach (string v in names)
            {
                object vv =
Registry.ClassesRoot.OpenSubKey(path).GetValue(v);
                RegistryValueKind vk =
Registry.ClassesRoot.OpenSubKey(path).GetValueKind(v);
                switch (vk)
                {
                    case RegistryValueKind.String:
                        {
                            name = v;
                            nk = "REG_SZ";
                            value = vv.ToString();
                            break;
                        }
                    case RegistryValueKind.ExpandString:
                        {
                            name = v;
                            nk = "REG_Expand_SZ";
                            value = vv.ToString();
                            break;
                        }
                    case RegistryValueKind.MultiString:
                        {
                            name = v;
                            nk = "REG_MULTI_SZ";
                            string[] mchammer = (string[])vv;
                            value = "";
                            for (int i = 0; i <
mchammer.GetLength(0); i++)
                            {
                                if (value != "")
                                {
                                    value = value + ", ";
```

```csharp
                            }
                            value = value +
mchammer.GetValue(i).ToString();
                            }
                            break;
                    }
                case RegistryValueKind.DWord:
                    {
                        name = v;
                        nk = "REG_DWORD";
                        int l = (int)vv;
                        value = "(0x" + l.ToString("X8") + ")
" + l.ToString();

                        break;
                    }
                case RegistryValueKind.QWord:
                    {
                        name = v;
                        nk = "REG_QWORD";
                        int l = (int)vv;
                        value = "(0x" + l.ToString("X8") + ")
" + l.ToString();

                        break;
                    }
                case RegistryValueKind.Binary:
                    {
                        byte[] bi = (byte[])vv;
                        name = v;
                        nk = "REG_BINARY";
                        string tempstr = "";
                        int len = bi.Length;
                        for (int i = 0; i < len; i++)
                        {
                            tempstr = bi[i].ToString("x");
                            if (tempstr.Length == 1)
                            {
                                tempstr = "0" + tempstr;
                            }
                            value = value + tempstr + " ";
                            tempstr = "";
                        }
                        break;
                    }

            }
```

```
                if (v == "")
                {
                    name = "(Default)";
                }
                txtstream.WriteLine("<tr>");
                txtstream.WriteLine("    <td align=\"left\">" +
name + "</td>");
                txtstream.WriteLine("    <td align=\"left\">" +
nk + "</td>");
                txtstream.WriteLine("    <td align=\"left\">" +
value + "</td>");
                txtstream.WriteLine("</tr>");

            }
            txtstream.WriteLine("</table>");
            txtstream.WriteLine("</body>");
            txtstream.WriteLine("</html>");
            txtstream.Close();


webBrowser1.Navigate(System.Environment.CurrentDirectory + "\\" +
comboBox1.Text + ".html");
            }

    }
}
```

Below is a screen shot:

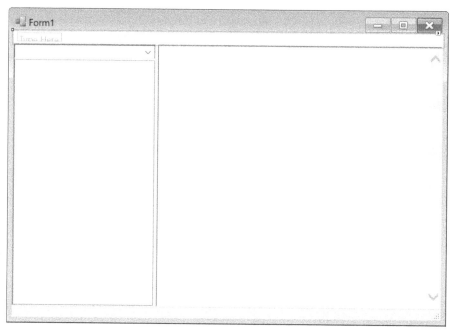

The layout consists of a MenuStrip, StatusStrip, two splitters, a combobox, a TreeView and a webBroswer. You can lay it out anyway you want. I just created it for the book and demo purposes.

The program in action:

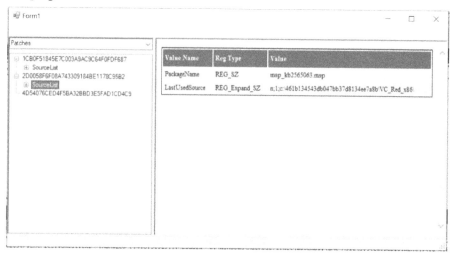

REMOTE REGISTRY CAPABILITIES

In both 32-bit and 64-bit versions

Aside from being able to produce HTML pages that can be saved for comparison for changes in the registry, you can also use the same code I've provided you with and repurpose it to run on a remote machine.

The beauty of this is that knowing how to use these features means you can do things with your registry code. And that makes you a valuable asset in the minds of your fellow employees and your boss.

So, it is kind of important that you understand what the code does and why it might fail under certain circumstances.

With that said, I also decided to streamline the chaos to passing in the type of hive I'm wanting to connect to, listed below:

```
RegistryHive.ClassesRoot
RegistryHive.CurrentConfig
RegistryHive.CurrentUser
RegistryHive.DynData
RegistryHive.LocalMachine
RegistryHive.PerformanceData
RegistryHive.Users
```

Then, pass in the ComputerName and tell the function what type of view I wanted to return. Those three variables are:

```
RegistryView.Registry32
RegistryView.Registry64
RegistryView.Default
```

While the code shown below looks like a lot of work, it wasn't. In fact, it took me longer to explain it then to write it. I also never have to write it again. I like that.

```csharp
private RegistryKey Open_Remote_Base_Key(String rh, string CN, string rv)
{
    RegistryKey regkey = null;

    switch (rh)
    {
        case "ClassesRoot":
        {
            switch (rv)
            {

                case "32":
                {
                    regkey = RegistryKey.OpenRemoteBaseKey(RegistryHive.ClassesRoot, CN,
RegistryView.Registry32);
                    break;
                }
                case "64":
                {
                    regkey = RegistryKey.OpenRemoteBaseKey(RegistryHive.ClassesRoot, CN,
RegistryView.Registry64);
                    break;
                }
                case "Default":
                {
                    regkey = RegistryKey.OpenRemoteBaseKey(RegistryHive.ClassesRoot, CN,
RegistryView.Default);
                    break;
                }
            }
            break;
        }
        case "CurrentConfig":
        {
            switch (rv)
            {

                case "32":
                {
                    regkey = RegistryKey.OpenRemoteBaseKey(RegistryHive.CurrentConfig, CN,
RegistryView.Registry32);
                    break;
                }
                case "64":
                {
                    regkey = RegistryKey.OpenRemoteBaseKey(RegistryHive.CurrentConfig, CN,
RegistryView.Registry64);
```

```
                    break;
                }
            case "Default":
                {
                    regkey = RegistryKey.OpenRemoteBaseKey(RegistryHive.CurrentConfig, CN,
RegistryView.Default);
                    break;
                }
        }
        break;
    }
case "CurrentUser":
    {
        switch (rv)
        {

            case "32":
                {
                    regkey = RegistryKey.OpenRemoteBaseKey(RegistryHive.CurrentUser, CN,
RegistryView.Registry32);
                    break;
                }
            case "64":
                {
                    regkey = RegistryKey.OpenRemoteBaseKey(RegistryHive.CurrentUser, CN,
RegistryView.Registry64);
                    break;
                }
            case "Default":
                {
                    regkey = RegistryKey.OpenRemoteBaseKey(RegistryHive.CurrentUser, CN,
RegistryView.Default);
                    break;
                }
        }
        break;
    }
case "DynData":
    {
        switch (rv)
        {

            case "32":
                {
                    regkey = RegistryKey.OpenRemoteBaseKey(RegistryHive.DynData, CN,
RegistryView.Registry32);
                    break;
                }
            case "64":
                {
                    regkey = RegistryKey.OpenRemoteBaseKey(RegistryHive.DynData, CN,
RegistryView.Registry64);
                    break;
                }
            case "Default":
                {
                    regkey = RegistryKey.OpenRemoteBaseKey(RegistryHive.DynData, CN,
RegistryView.Default);
                    break;
                }
        }
        break;
    }
case "LocalMachine":
    {
        switch (rv)
```

```csharp
                            {
                case "32":
                    {
                        regkey = RegistryKey.OpenRemoteBaseKey(RegistryHive.LocalMachine, CN,
RegistryView.Registry32);
                        break;
                    }
                case "64":
                    {
                        regkey = RegistryKey.OpenRemoteBaseKey(RegistryHive.LocalMachine, CN,
RegistryView.Registry64);
                        break;
                    }
                case "Default":
                    {
                        regkey = RegistryKey.OpenRemoteBaseKey(RegistryHive.LocalMachine, CN,
RegistryView.Default);
                        break;
                    }
            }
            break;
        }
    case "PerformanceData":
        {
            switch (rv)
            {
                case "32":
                    {
                        regkey = RegistryKey.OpenRemoteBaseKey(RegistryHive.PerformanceData, CN,
RegistryView.Registry32);
                        break;
                    }
                case "64":
                    {
                        regkey = RegistryKey.OpenRemoteBaseKey(RegistryHive.PerformanceData, CN,
RegistryView.Registry64);
                        break;
                    }
                case "Default":
                    {
                        regkey = RegistryKey.OpenRemoteBaseKey(RegistryHive.PerformanceData, CN,
RegistryView.Default);
                        break;
                    }
            }
            break;
        }
    case "Users":
        {
            switch (rv)
            {
                case "32":
                    {
                        regkey = RegistryKey.OpenRemoteBaseKey(RegistryHive.Users, CN,
RegistryView.Registry32);
                        break;
                    }
                case "64":
                    {
                        regkey = RegistryKey.OpenRemoteBaseKey(RegistryHive.Users, CN,
RegistryView.Registry64);
                        break;
                    }
```

```
        case "Default":
            {
                regkey = RegistryKey.OpenRemoteBaseKey(RegistryHive.Users, CN, RegistryView.Default);
                break;
            }
        }
        break;
    }
}
return regkey;
}
```

I want to emphasize the importance of streamlining reusable code. All too often you will go into a job where the code needed to get the project off the ground is the same code.

After you've spent as much time as I have writing code, you come to realize that almost all of the .Net coding conventions can be put into routines that can be written in such a way that at a press of a button, you can create much of the code needed to complete a project.

The above code is not an example of this. It could be if it was being written out by another program. But it is an example of a function that should be mass produced because it is a routine I nor you should have to write over and over again.

I can't tell you how much time it will save you to think and write up your routines for common code subs and functions. But if it took me 10 minutes to write the above code, pressing the button to reproduce it for another project would take less than a second. Based on purely those two numbers and not on your ability to type like Clark Kent, it comes out to 600 times faster without typos.

I'm not perfect, I'm human. The computer isn't human, but it is a heck of a lot faster and types a heck of a lot better than I do. Furthermore, if your computer is only 8 times faster – which it isn't (it would have to be using an 8080 processor with the slowest memory and hard drive ever built) - in one hour it is going to produce 8 hours' worth of code.

It is more like in 5 minutes for 8 hours.

Anyway, the coding we've been using so far has shown that the filtering of registry DataTypes for dealing with ValueNames, ValueKinds and Values is one of those routines you could use over and over again, too.

There's a lot to think about.

WRITING REGISTRY CODE FOR DATA MINING AND SPECIFIC END USER REQUESTS

When all bets are off

How many times have you worked on code thinking, gee, this looks familiar and then realize that you hadn't thought of using it that way?

How many times have I though a general routine I cooked up turned out to be a really bad idea? Why does this happen?

There's actually a pretty simple answer that when you're not on deadline you look back and realize why you code just didn't blend or conform to what the customer wanted done.

It is called blind side notation – which is another way of saying, "I didn't that one coming."

A piece of code serves a purpose. But that same piece of code just might need a bit of help doing it. And that's where code logic that works great to complete a task fails miserably a doing it elsewhere.

So, what does stop a piece of code from working?

A mile-high analyst would suggest permissions while an experienced coder would probably mumble something like, "If coding were easy, they would hire chimpanzees."

Well somewhere in between is the real truth and it boils down to if and then steps which funnel the variables down to where the single piece of logic will work every time no matter what.

By the way, it is called experience. You know, the thing you put on your resume? The thing they can teach in school, either. The military likes using boots on the ground. I prefer to call it the eyes on the issue. Here's an example.

The statement of work (SOW) defines what you will be doing and how long it should take to get the job done. As a contractor, that is what you agree to do while working for your customer. It's also the result of matching your skills when head-hunters look at your resume as being a match for what needs to be done.

Anytime the SOW goes off the reservation, the effect of it is called scope creep.

Now, that's a general overview and a lot of assumptions that are not covered in the SOW that prove to be false also have an affect on the timeline needed to complete the job.

Often, this boils down to you putting more time in but not getting paid for it. And I don't know about you but when these things happen and it is not my fault, there is no excuse why I shouldn't get paid to finish the job.

I know of no other profession in the world that works this way. Estimates are just that. You certainly would want to pay more if an honest vehicle repair person told you that he had to replace the break lines because they were showing signs of wear and tear, were leaking and could fail without notice.

And yet, when we go to work for a customer we are on a timeline that doesn't consider blocking issues that were obviously there all along like those issues are our fault.

When you see code that you know should be working but it doesn't, that is the first sign that there is a silent, built in resistance to coding in standard best practice routines and procedures.

Suppose for a minute, you needed to test this piece of remote registry code:

```
RegistryKey regkey = null;
Regkey = RegistryKey.OpenRemoteBaseKey(RegistryHive.ClassesRoot, CN,
RegistryView.Registry32);
```

You are told that a remote computer was setup in the server room so you could connect to it from your development machine for testing. You are given the name of the computer by the manager of the team you are working for.

If you had this code up when the manager handed you the name of the computer, you could type the computer name into the routine and test it right then and there. If it didn't work, the manager would have to go and figure out why.

If you try running it after he walked away, you would start questioning your skills at writing it. In fact, you would most likely test it on your local machine:

```
Regkey = RegistryKey.OpenRemoteBaseKey(RegistryHive.ClassesRoot, "",
RegistryView.Registry32);
```

If it failed then, you'd start wondering what you are doing wrong. We all do this. It is human nature. But I'm here to tell you that there is nothing wrong with this line of code...unless there is a security policy, permissions issue, a blocked port or a remote machine that isn't on the same domain as your development machine.

An hour later, you finally get up the nerve to talk to that manager and the problem gets resolved. Your log in account doesn't give you domain level permissions and a policy is in play that says no one without domain level administrator privileges can read or write to the registry.

You just spent the whole entire day not only questioning your ability to code but worrying about something that should have been resolved long before you sat down and started writing code.

Experience builds confidence. It also helps to know what permissions you have and if that is going to have any impact on you getting your job done.

If you get an access denied on just trying to run this:

Regkey = RegistryKey.OpenRemoteBaseKey(RegistryHive.ClassesRoot, "",
RegistryView.Registry32);

Then I seriously doubt that you're going to gain access to a remote computer's registry either. First, find out what group you are in with respect to your level or permissions.

Log into the remote machine. Once logged in on the remote computer, go to Start, right click on the start icon, and select run, type in regedit and then click the ok button. Expand the HKEY_LOCAL_MACHINE hive. The Expand System, CurrentControlSet, Control and SecurePipeServices subkeys. Expanding SecurePipeServices will expose the winreg subkey.

Right click on winreg and click on permissions. If you or the group isn't in the list, you can't connect to that computer's registry. I just added everyone full control on my other machine. Let's see if that works:

```
using System;
using System.Collections.Generic;
using System.ComponentModel;
using System.Data;
using System.Drawing;
using System.Linq;
using System.Text;
using System.Windows.Forms;
using System.Management;
using Microsoft.Win32;
namespace WindowsFormsApplication3
{
    public partial class Form1 : Form
    {
        public Form1()
        {
            InitializeComponent();
        }

        private void Form1_Load(object sender, EventArgs e)
```

```
    {
        RegistryKey Regkey =
RegistryKey.OpenRemoteBaseKey(RegistryHive.ClassesRoot,
"192.168.0.99", RegistryView.Registry32);
        string[] names = Regkey.GetSubKeyNames();
        MessageBox.Show(names.GetLength(0).ToString());

    }
  }
}
```

Results:

By the way, using tracert at the command line or through PowerShell, and use the Machine Name, I get the IP6 address: fe80::b11c:1b81:df90:d987%7

Even after I put everyone into the permissions and then use the computer name, I get the below message.

Same thing happens when I use the IP6 address I get the same error.

But the code works when I use the IP4 address and without adding everyone. Apparently, I missed a step. Here's the link that will talk you through what to look for and do.

So, now, at this point, assuming it is just a problem with passing credentials across to the other machine, even if that is the only problem right now, you really do need to make sure that is the real problem and not something else.

So, you bring up Regedit on your development box, go to the top of Regedit's menu, click on Connect Network Registry. An Active Directory window will open.

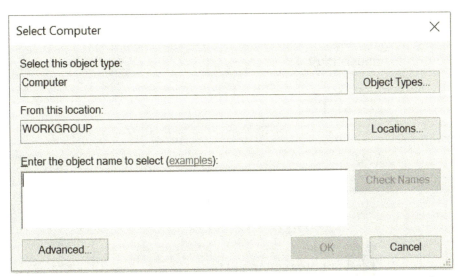

When you remoted over to the machine you've been told to test your registry code on, find out what the machine's IP address is. On that machine, go to start, right click on it, select run, type in cmd in the text box and click OK. Then type in the cmd console, IPConfig and press enter. Find the machines IP Address, write it down and close the window and sign out of the remote session.

Type in that IP address and click okay.

A log on screen will appear. Type in the credentials you used to log in remotely and click okay.

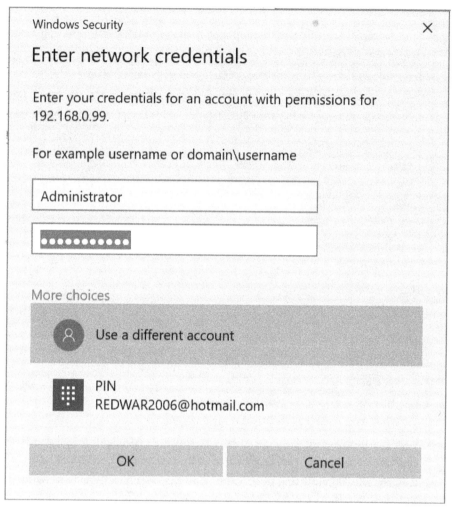

Windows Security   ✕

Enter network credentials

Enter your credentials for an account with permissions for 192.168.0.99.

For example username or domain\username

| Administrator |

| •••••••••••• |

More choices

   ⊗   Use a different account

   ⊞   PIN
        REDWAR2006@hotmail.com

| OK | Cancel |

After you have done this, you should see something like this show up in regedit:

Registry Editor

File Edit View Favorites Help

192.168.0.99

- ∨ 💻 Computer
  - › ▥ HKEY_CLASSES_ROOT
  - › ▥ HKEY_CURRENT_USER
  - › ▥ HKEY_LOCAL_MACHINE
  - › ▥ HKEY_USERS
  - › ▥ HKEY_CURRENT_CONFIG
- ∨ 🌐 192.168.0.99
  - › ▥ HKEY_LOCAL_MACHINE
  - › ▥ HKEY_USERS

Okay, so, if we know this works, shouldn't your remote code work?

Well, all incoming objects from a remote machine to the target machine goes through DCOM to verify username and password and to confirm the credentials of the person making the call.

Once all of this happens, the two computers talk on a port number between 1024 through 65535. You can bet having firewalls between the two machines can cause issues, too.

There are a couple of COM and .Net ways you can connect to a remote registry other than the leap of faith Active Directory domain connected machines use. Below is one of them. The code below is

```
SWbemLocator L = new SWbemLocator();
SWbemServices svc = L.ConnectServer("192.168.0.99", "root\\Default", "UserName", "Password", "MS-0409");
SWbemObject obj = svc.Get("StdRegProv", 0, null);

int v = 0;

SWbemObject inparams = obj.Methods_.Item("EnumKey").InParameters;
inparams.Properties_.Item("hDefKey", 0).set_Value(0x80000002);
inparams.Properties_.Item("sSubKeyName",
0).set_Value("SOFTWARE\\WOW6432Node\\Classes\\CLSID");
SWbemObject outParams = obj.ExecMethod_("EnumKey", inparams);
Object[] Names = outParams.Properties_.Item("sNames").get_Value();
Console.Out.WriteLine(Names.GetLength(0));
```

This is similar code running on the machine I am trying to connect to, and both come back with the same amount of subkeys: 5240

```
String[] names =
Registry.LocalMachine.OpenSubKey("Software\\WOW6432Node\\Classes\\CLSID").GetSubKeyNames();
    Console.Out.WriteLine(Names.GetLength(0));
```

The point to all of this is simple. If the credentials work on the machine which you can't currently connect to and you are able to do the same with Regedit, then you know it isn't your code that is not working, but the permissions between the machines.

You can also see, based on what his being displayed in Regedit that not all of the registry hives are made available for you to view from a remote machine.

When I connected to my remote machine using Regedit, I was only able to look at HKEY_LOCAL_MACHINE and HKEY_USERS. If these to hives are the only two you need to work with then, you're fine. Otherwise, you're probably going to need the help from the Administrator to fix what can or can't be seen from a remote connection.

PROVIDERS, DRIVERS AND ISAMS

Weren't you waiting for the Oh, my?

Well, I wasn't. It just sounded corky enough to add to this subtitle.

In this chapter, we're going to be focusing on looking for specific things. Yes, we did already cover how to enumerate though the registry entries but that was using filter if statements know I've found one. This time, we're not going through all the program IDs -ProgIDs – first. Instead, we're using:

```
RegistryKey regkey = Registry.LocalMachine.OpenSubKey("Software\\WOW6432Node\\Classes\\CLSID\\" + n + "\\Ole Db Provider");
```

If this key is not null then we know we've found one. Also, since I know the registry value kind is a string and has no name value, I simply add the not null key's string value to the listbox.

Let's take a look at what I'm seeing in the registry.

r:\HKEY_LOCAL_MACHINE\SOFTWARE\WOW6432Node\Classes\CLSID\{0C7FF16C-38E3-11d0-97AB-00C04FC2AD98}\OLE DB Provider

	Name	Type	Data
> {0C7EFBDE-0303-4c6f-A4F7-31FA2BE5E397}	(Default)	REG_SZ	Microsoft OLE DB Provider for SQL Server
∨ {0C7FF16C-38E3-11d0-97AB-00C04FC2AD98}			
> ExtendedErrors			
> Implemented Categories			
InprocServer32			
OLE DB Provider			
ProgID			
VersionIndependentProgID			

The subkey: OLE DB Provider is there and the value I'm wanting to add to my list of providers. I know the registry value kind is a string and has no name value, I simply add the not null key's data type is REG_SZ. So adding it to the listbox is simply a getValue("") call. Below is the code.

```
using System;
using System.Collections.Generic;
using System.ComponentModel;
using System.Data;
using System.Drawing;
using System.Linq;
using System.Text;
using System.Windows.Forms;
using Microsoft.Win32;
namespace WindowsFormsApplication1
{
    public partial class Form1 : Form
    {
        public Form1()
        {
            InitializeComponent();
        }

        private void Form1_Load(object sender, EventArgs e)
        {
            string[] names =
Registry.LocalMachine.OpenSubKey("Software\\WOW6432Node\\Classes\\CLSID").GetSubKeyNames();

            foreach (string n in names)
            {
                RegistryKey regkey =
Registry.LocalMachine.OpenSubKey("Software\\WOW6432Node\\Classes\\CLSID\\"
+ n + "\\OLE DB Provider");
                if (regkey != null)
                {
                    listBox1.Items.Add(regkey.GetValue(""));
                }
            }
        }
    }
}
```

The results look like this:

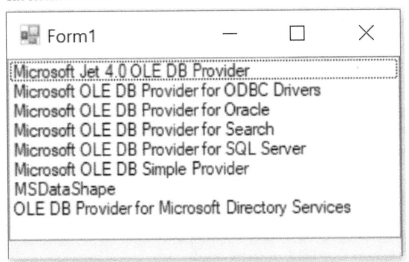

Want to know another secret? The Datalinks does the same thing. So, if we wanted to see how close our registry code is to what the DataLinks sees, we would write the following code:

```csharp
using System;
using System.Collections.Generic;
using System.ComponentModel;
using System.Data;
using System.Drawing;
using System.Linq;
using System.Text;
using System.Windows.Forms;
using ADODB;
using MSDASC;
namespace WindowsFormsApplication2
{
    public partial class Form1 : Form
    {
        public Form1()
        {
            InitializeComponent();
        }

        private void Form1_Load(object sender, EventArgs e)
```

```
        {
            ADODB.Connection cn = new ADODB.Connection();
            MSDASC.DataLinks dl = new MSDASC.DataLinks();
            cn = dl.PromptNew();
        }
    }
}
```
Looks like we found all of them:

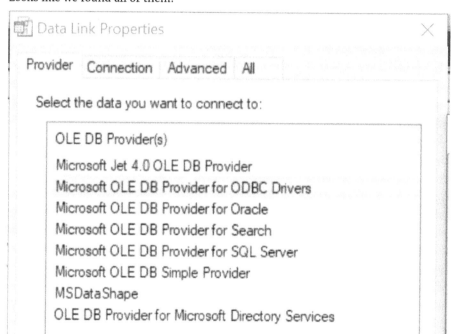

Before we move on, I need to tell you that you have to add a COM ADO reference: Microsoft ActiveX Data Objects to the project. And add another reference which you will browse over to and that's: *C:\Program Files\Common Files\System\Ole DB\OLEDB32.DLL*. After you've done that, add then use the code I just used to create the list.

What about running the same code in 64-bit? Well, after telling the compiler to run in 64-bit mode, the code still returned the 32-bit providers. So we're going to change where the registry code should go to look:

```csharp
using System;
using System.Collections.Generic;
using System.ComponentModel;
using System.Data;
using System.Drawing;
using System.Linq;
using System.Text;
using System.Windows.Forms;
using Microsoft.Win32;
namespace WindowsFormsApplication1
{
    public partial class Form1 : Form
    {
        public Form1()
        {
            InitializeComponent();
        }

        private void Form1_Load(object sender, EventArgs e)
        {
            string[] names =
Registry.LocalMachine.OpenSubKey("Software\\Classes\\CLSID").GetSubKeyNames()
;

            foreach (string n in names)
            {
                RegistryKey regkey =
Registry.LocalMachine.OpenSubKey("Software\\Classes\\CLSID\\" + n + "\\Ole Db
Provider");
                if (regkey != null)
                {
                    listBox1.Items.Add(regkey.GetValue(""));
                }
            }
        }
    }
}
```

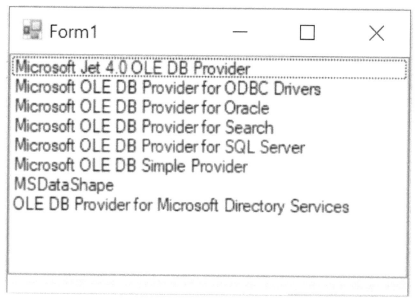

As expected, it is a much smaller list. But let's keep leaving out the WOW6432Node and reset the compiler to 32=mode:

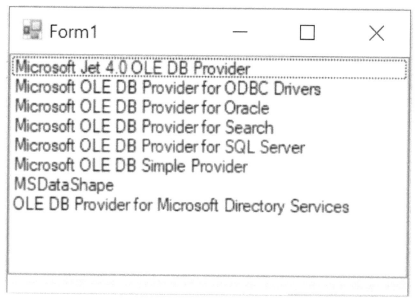

So, what did we just discover? Well, if we don't add the WOW6432Node, using the compile settings to either 32-bit or 64-bit, we get the providers for 32-bit and we get the 64-bit providers for 64-bit.

However, if we do use the WOW6432Node registry key, even if we change the compiler to 64-bit, we still go to the 32-bit providers.

While that may sound like it is broken, this behavior actually makes a lot of sense.

Suppose you want to install a 32-bit program on a 64-bit machine. If the 32-bit installer is used and the software was designed to install in Software\Classes directory, having the ability to know the 32-bit software really needed to register itself in the Software\WOW6432Node instead.

On the other hand if a 64-bit program also has support for 32-bit programs as well, it could specify registry entries for both Software and Software\WOW6432Node and the registry entries for a seamless install.

Of course, you wouldn't have known this had you not tried the code or, at the very least, seen me go through the process of showing you that this is the behavior demonstrated in the code examples.

Bottom line here, 64-bit can read both 32-bit keys and 64-bit keys but when you use the same flexibility using the 32-bit compiler options, you will on see the 32-bit registry entries.

FRIENDLY NAMES VERSES WHAT IS NEEDED TO CREATE OBJECT

As you saw with the code using the datalinks, we could check and see if we found the same names as what the datalinks found.

But those are what is known as friendly names and in code, we can't create objects or connection strings with them. Since there are less than 20 of them, why don't we expand the information so we can do something useful with the code.

In fact, what we're going to do is add a DataGridView to the form. Create a column for the – in this case = 64-bit provider's ClassID, file location and name, friendly name, ProgID and VersionIndependentProgID if there is one.

The code starts on the next page.

```
using System;
using System.Collections.Generic;
using System.ComponentModel;
using System.Data;
using System.Drawing;
```

```csharp
using System.Linq;
using System.Text;
using System.Threading.Tasks;
using System.Windows.Forms;
using Microsoft.Win32;

namespace WindowsFormsApp1
{
    public partial class Form1 : Form
    {
        public Form1()
        {
            InitializeComponent();
        }

        private void Form1_Load(object sender, EventArgs e)
        {

            dataGridView1.Columns.Add("ClassID", "ClassID");
            dataGridView1.Columns.Add("Filename", "Filename");
            dataGridView1.Columns.Add("User Friendly Name", "User Friendly Name");
            dataGridView1.Columns.Add("ProgID", "ProgID");
            dataGridView1.Columns.Add("VersionIndependentProgID",
"VersionIndependentProgID");

            int x = 0;
            string[] names =
Registry.LocalMachine.OpenSubKey("Software\\Classes\\CLSID").GetSubKeyNames()
;

                foreach (string n in names)
                {
                    RegistryKey regkey =
Registry.LocalMachine.OpenSubKey("Software\\Classes\\CLSID\\" + n + "\\Ole Db
Provider");
                    if (regkey != null)
                    {
                    dataGridView1.Rows.Add();
                    dataGridView1.Rows[x].Cells[0].Value = n;
                    dataGridView1.Rows[x].Cells[1].Value =
Registry.LocalMachine.OpenSubKey("Software\\Classes\\CLSID\\" + n +
"\\InProcServer32").GetValue("");
                        dataGridView1.Rows[x].Cells[2].Value =
Registry.LocalMachine.OpenSubKey("Software\\Classes\\CLSID\\" + n + "\\Ole Db
Provider").GetValue("");
                        dataGridView1.Rows[x].Cells[3].Value =
Registry.LocalMachine.OpenSubKey("Software\\Classes\\CLSID\\" + n +
"\\ProgID").GetValue("");
                        try
                        {
```

```
                dataGridView1.Rows[x].Cells[4].Value =
Registry.LocalMachine.OpenSubKey("Software\\Classes\\CLSID\\" + n +
"\\VersionIndependentProgID").GetValue("");
                }
                catch(Exception ex)
                {

                }
                x = x + 1;
            }
        }

dataGridView1.AutoResizeColumns(DataGridViewAutoSizeColumnsMode.AllCells);
        }
    }
}
```

Here's the output:

When we switch this to use the 32-bit complier with the same code, it produces this:

At this point, we can add code to this to populate file info and version info for each one of these providers.

However, we have a lot of other code examples I want to cover that I think you're going to want to learn how to do.

THE LIFE AND TIMES OF REGISTERED COM CLASSES

The code we just used in the previous chapter is very similar to what we could use to enumerate through the registry entries and look for keys with ProgIDs.

That kind of thinking presents some issues.

In the first place, unless you know what registry entries are controls, providers or some new entry that doesn't have a ProgID or a VersionIndependentProgID, well, you're going to find it pretty hard to code.

Furthermore, I am not doing anything with my code to create entries or delete them. I have chosen this approach because if you don't know what you are doing you could easily end up having to rebuild your machine and I have no intention of being sued.

So, I've taken a more read only approach to the coding examples. Even at that, there are some rather elaborate coding routines which are very detailed and unique to the way I address custom views of the registry.

For example, the values of a specific registry entry are all done in HTML.

Value Name	Reg Type	Value
Driver da Microsoft para arquivos texto (*.txt; *.csv)	REG_SZ	Installed
Driver do Microsoft Access (*.mdb)	REG_SZ	Installed
Driver do Microsoft dBase (*.dbf)	REG_SZ	Installed
Driver do Microsoft Excel(*.xls)	REG_SZ	Installed
Driver do Microsoft Paradox (*.db)	REG_SZ	Installed
Microsoft Access Driver (*.mdb)	REG_SZ	Installed
Microsoft Access-Treiber (*.mdb)	REG_SZ	Installed
Microsoft dBase Driver (*.dbf)	REG_SZ	Installed
Microsoft dBase-Treiber (*.dbf)	REG_SZ	Installed
Microsoft Excel Driver (*.xls)	REG_SZ	Installed
Microsoft Excel-Treiber (*.xls)	REG_SZ	Installed
Microsoft ODBC for Oracle	REG_SZ	Installed
Microsoft Paradox Driver (*.db)	REG_SZ	Installed
Microsoft Paradox-Treiber (*.db)	REG_SZ	Installed
Microsoft Text Driver (*.txt; *.csv)	REG_SZ	Installed
Microsoft Text-Treiber (*.txt; *.csv)	REG_SZ	Installed
SQL Server	REG_SZ	Installed
Microsoft ODBC Driver for Oracle	REG_SZ	Installed
ODBC Driver 17 for SQL Server	REG_SZ	Installed

So, when I find something that makes it easier for you to be able to know what is going on under the hood, I will provide you with the code that targets those specific entries and you can see for yourself the specific code needed to display it and get the same results.

In the case of the displayed ODBC drivers, the below code will produce this view:

The key we need to open is:

SOFTWARE\WOW6432Node\ODBC\ODBCINST.INI\ODBC Drivers.

The code needs to COM references: Microsoft Scripting Runtime and Microsoft.Win32.

```
using System;
using System.Collections.Generic;
using System.ComponentModel;
using System.Data;
using System.Drawing;
using System.Linq;
using System.Text;
using System.Threading.Tasks;
using System.Windows.Forms;
using Microsoft.Win32;
using Scripting;

namespace WindowsFormsApp4
{
    public partial class Form1 : Form
    {
        public Form1()
        {
            InitializeComponent();
        }

        private void Form1_Load(object sender, EventArgs e)
        {
```

```csharp
            RegistryKey                        regKey                        =
Registry.LocalMachine.OpenSubKey("SOFTWARE\\WOW6432Node\\ODBC\\ODBCINS
T.INI\\ODBC Drivers");
        string[] vname = regKey.GetValueNames();
        string name = "";
        string nk = "";
        string value = "";

        FileSystemObject fso = new FileSystemObject();
            TextStream                        txtstream                        =
fso.OpenTextFile(System.Environment.CurrentDirectory    +    "\\Registry.html",
IOMode.ForWriting, true, Tristate.TristateUseDefault);
        txtstream.WriteLine("<hmtl>");
        txtstream.WriteLine("<head>");
        txtstream.WriteLine("<title></title>");
        txtstream.WriteLine("<style type=text/css>");
        txtstream.WriteLine("#itsthetable {");
        txtstream.WriteLine("       font-family: Georgia, \"Times New Roman\",
Times, serif;");
        txtstream.WriteLine("       color: #036;");
        txtstream.WriteLine("}");

        txtstream.WriteLine("caption {");
        txtstream.WriteLine("       font-size: 48px;");
        txtstream.WriteLine("       color: #036;");
        txtstream.WriteLine("       font-weight: bolder;");
        txtstream.WriteLine("       font-variant: small-caps;");
        txtstream.WriteLine("}");

        txtstream.WriteLine("th {");
        txtstream.WriteLine("       font-size: 12px;");
        txtstream.WriteLine("       color: #FFF;");
        txtstream.WriteLine("       background-color: #06C;");
```

```
txtstream.WriteLine("          padding: 8px 4px;");
txtstream.WriteLine("          border-bottom: 1px solid #015ebc;");
txtstream.WriteLine("}");

txtstream.WriteLine("table {");
txtstream.WriteLine("          margin: 0;");
txtstream.WriteLine("          padding: 0;");
txtstream.WriteLine("          border-collapse: collapse;");
txtstream.WriteLine("          border: 1px solid #06C;");
txtstream.WriteLine("          width: 100%");
txtstream.WriteLine("}");

txtstream.WriteLine("#itsthetable th a:link, #itsthetable th a:visited {");
txtstream.WriteLine("          color: #FFF;");
txtstream.WriteLine("          text-decoration: none;");
txtstream.WriteLine("          border-left: 5px solid #FFF;");
txtstream.WriteLine("          padding-left: 3px;");
txtstream.WriteLine("}");

txtstream.WriteLine("th a:hover, #itsthetable th a:active {");
txtstream.WriteLine("          color: #F90;");
txtstream.WriteLine("          text-decoration: line-through;");
txtstream.WriteLine("          border-left: 5px solid #F90;");
txtstream.WriteLine("          padding-left: 3px;");
txtstream.WriteLine("}");

txtstream.WriteLine("tbody th:hover {");
txtstream.WriteLine("          background-image:
url(imgs/tbody_hover.gif);");
txtstream.WriteLine("          background-position: bottom;");
txtstream.WriteLine("          background-repeat: repeat-x;");
txtstream.WriteLine("}");
```

```
txtstream.WriteLine("td {");
txtstream.WriteLine("        background-color: #f2f2f2;");
txtstream.WriteLine("        padding: 4px;");
txtstream.WriteLine("        font-size: 12px;");
txtstream.WriteLine("}");

txtstream.WriteLine("#itsthetable td:hover {");
txtstream.WriteLine("        background-color: #f8f8f8;");

txtstream.WriteLine("}");

txtstream.WriteLine("#itsthetable td a:link, #itsthetable td a:visited {");
txtstream.WriteLine("        color: #039;");
txtstream.WriteLine("        text-decoration: none;");
txtstream.WriteLine("        border-left: 3px solid #039;");
txtstream.WriteLine("        padding-left: 3px;");
txtstream.WriteLine("}");

txtstream.WriteLine("#itsthetable td a:hover, #itsthetable td a:active {");
txtstream.WriteLine("        color: #06C;");
txtstream.WriteLine("        text-decoration: line-through;");
txtstream.WriteLine("        border-left: 3px solid #06C;");
txtstream.WriteLine("        padding-left: 3px;");
txtstream.WriteLine("}");

txtstream.WriteLine("#itsthetable th {");
txtstream.WriteLine("        text-align: left;");
txtstream.WriteLine("        width: 150px;");
txtstream.WriteLine("}");

txtstream.WriteLine("#itsthetable tr {");
txtstream.WriteLine("        border-bottom: 1px solid #CCC;");
txtstream.WriteLine("}");
```

```
txtstream.WriteLine("#itsthetable thead th {");
txtstream.WriteLine("        background-image: url(imgs/thead_back.gif);");
txtstream.WriteLine("        background-repeat: repeat-x;");
txtstream.WriteLine("        background-color: #06C;");
txtstream.WriteLine("        height: 30px;");
txtstream.WriteLine("        font-size: 18px;");
txtstream.WriteLine("        text-align: center;");
txtstream.WriteLine("        text-shadow: #333 2px 2px;");
txtstream.WriteLine("        border: 2px;");
txtstream.WriteLine("}");

txtstream.WriteLine("#itsthetable tfoot th {");
txtstream.WriteLine("        background-image: url(imgs/tfoot_back.gif);");
txtstream.WriteLine("        background-repeat: repeat-x;");
txtstream.WriteLine("        background-color: #036;");
txtstream.WriteLine("        height: 30px;");
txtstream.WriteLine("        font-size: 28px;");
txtstream.WriteLine("        text-align: center;");
txtstream.WriteLine("        text-shadow: #333 2px 2px;");
txtstream.WriteLine("}");

txtstream.WriteLine("#itsthetable tfoot td {");
txtstream.WriteLine("        background-image: url(imgs/tfoot_back.gif);");
txtstream.WriteLine("        background-repeat: repeat-x;");
txtstream.WriteLine("        background-color: #036;");
txtstream.WriteLine("        color: FFF;");
txtstream.WriteLine("        height: 30px;");
txtstream.WriteLine("        font-size: 24px;");
txtstream.WriteLine("        text-align: left;");
txtstream.WriteLine("        text-shadow: #333 2px 2px;");
txtstream.WriteLine("}");
```

```csharp
txtstream.WriteLine("tbody td a[href=\"http://www.csslab.cl/\"] {");
txtstream.WriteLine("        font-weight: bolder;");
txtstream.WriteLine("}");
txtstream.WriteLine("</style>");
txtstream.WriteLine("<body>");
txtstream.WriteLine("<center>");
txtstream.WriteLine("<table Style=\"Border:0;\">");
txtstream.WriteLine("<tr><TH        Nowrap        STYLE=\"background-color:white;FONT-WEIGHT:normal; FONT-SIZE: 48px; COLOR: navy; FONT-STYLE: normal; FONT-FAMILY: Edwardian Script ITC\"></TH></tr>");
txtstream.WriteLine("</table>");
txtstream.WriteLine("<table                style=\"border:Double;border-width:1px;border-color:navy;\" cellpadding=2 cellspacing=2 Width=0>");
txtstream.WriteLine("<tr>");
txtstream.WriteLine("   <th align=\"left\">Value Name</th>");
txtstream.WriteLine("   <th align=\"left\">Reg Type</th>");
txtstream.WriteLine("   <th align=\"left\">Value</th>");
txtstream.WriteLine("</tr>");


foreach (string v in vname)
{
    object vv = regKey.GetValue(v);
    RegistryValueKind vk = regKey.GetValueKind(v);
    switch (vk)
    {
      case RegistryValueKind.String:
        {
          name = v;
          nk = "REG_SZ";
          value = vv.ToString();
          break;
        }
```

```csharp
                case RegistryValueKind.ExpandString:
                    {
                        name = v;
                        nk = "REG_Expand_SZ";
                        value = vv.ToString();
                        break;
                    }
                case RegistryValueKind.MultiString:
                    {
                        name = v;
                        nk = "REG_MULTI_SZ";
                        string[] mchammer = (string[])vv;
                        value = "";
                        for (int i = 0; i < mchammer.GetLength(0); i++)
                        {
                            if (value != "")
                            {
                                value = value + ", ";
                            }
                            value = value + mchammer.GetValue(i).ToString();
                        }
                        break;
                    }
                case RegistryValueKind.DWord:
                    {
                        name = v;
                        nk = "REG_DWORD";
                        int l = (int)vv;
                        value = "(0x" + l.ToString("X8") + ") " + l.ToString();
                        break;
                    }
                case RegistryValueKind.QWord:
                    {
```

```csharp
            name = v;
            nk = "REG_QWORD";
            int l = (int)vv;
            value = "(0x" + l.ToString("X8") + ") " + l.ToString();
            break;
        }
    case RegistryValueKind.Binary:
        {
            byte[] bi = (byte[])vv;
            name = v;
            nk = "REG_BINARY";
            string tempstr = "";
            int len = bi.Length;
            for (int i = 0; i < len; i++)
            {
                tempstr = bi[i].ToString("x");
                if (tempstr.Length == 1)
                {
                    tempstr = "0" + tempstr;
                }
                value = value + tempstr + " ";
                tempstr = "";
            }
            break;
        }

}
if (v == "")
{
    name = "(Default)";
}
txtstream.WriteLine("<tr>");
txtstream.WriteLine("   <td align=\"left\">" + name + "</td>");
```

```
        txtstream.WriteLine("    <td align=\"left\">" + nk + "</td>");
        txtstream.WriteLine("    <td align=\"left\">" + value + "</td>");
        txtstream.WriteLine("</tr>");

    }
    txtstream.WriteLine("</table>");
    txtstream.WriteLine("</body>");
    txtstream.WriteLine("</html>");
    txtstream.Close();

    webBrowser1.Navigate(System.Environment.CurrentDirectory        +
"\\Registry.html");
    }

  }
}
```

And that produces this:

Value Name	Reg Type	Value
Driver da Microsoft para arquivos texto (*.txt; *.csv)	REG_SZ	Installed
Driver do Microsoft Access (*.mdb)	REG_SZ	Installed
Driver do Microsoft dBase (*.dbf)	REG_SZ	Installed
Driver do Microsoft Excel(*.xls)	REG_SZ	Installed
Driver do Microsoft Paradox (*.db)	REG_SZ	Installed
Microsoft Access Driver (*.mdb)	REG_SZ	Installed
Microsoft Access-Treiber (*.mdb)	REG_SZ	Installed
Microsoft dBase Driver (*.dbf)	REG_SZ	Installed
Microsoft dBase-Treiber (*.dbf)	REG_SZ	Installed
Microsoft Excel Driver (*.xls)	REG_SZ	Installed
Microsoft Excel-Treiber (*.xls)	REG_SZ	Installed
Microsoft ODBC for Oracle	REG_SZ	Installed
Microsoft Paradox Driver (*.db)	REG_SZ	Installed
Microsoft Paradox-Treiber (*.db)	REG_SZ	Installed
Microsoft Text Driver (*.txt; *.csv)	REG_SZ	Installed
Microsoft Text-Treiber (*.txt; *.csv)	REG_SZ	Installed
SQL Server	REG_SZ	Installed
Microsoft ODBC Driver for Oracle	REG_SZ	Installed
ODBC Driver 17 for SQL Server	REG_SZ	Installed

Obviously, we can do this for a lot of informative registry but what about something like what ISAMS are installed?

Turns out those are collections of keys and all keys in the registry – according to the way things work using the .Net registry API = are all string values and come back as an array of string values.

```
using System;
using System.Collections.Generic;
using System.ComponentModel;
using System.Data;
using System.Drawing;
using System.Linq;
using System.Text;
using System.Threading.Tasks;
using System.Windows.Forms;
using Microsoft.Win32;
using Scripting;
```

```
namespace WindowsFormsApp4
{
    public partial class Form1 : Form
    {
        public Form1()
        {
            InitializeComponent();
        }

        private void Form1_Load(object sender, EventArgs e)
        {
            RegistryKey regKey =
Registry.LocalMachine.OpenSubKey("SOFTWARE\\WOW6432Node\\Microsoft\\Jet\\4
.0\\ISAM Formats");
            string[] vname = regKey.GetSubKeyNames();
            string name = "";
            string nk = "";
            string value = "";

            FileSystemObject fso = new FileSystemObject();
            TextStream txtstream =
fso.OpenTextFile(System.Environment.CurrentDirectory + "\\Registry.html",
IOMode.ForWriting, true, Tristate.TristateUseDefault);
            txtstream.WriteLine("<hmtl>");
            txtstream.WriteLine("<head>");
            txtstream.WriteLine("<title></title>");
            txtstream.WriteLine("<style type=text/css>");
            txtstream.WriteLine("#itsthetable {");
            txtstream.WriteLine("        font-family: Georgia, \"Times New Roman\",
Times, serif;");
            txtstream.WriteLine("        color: #036;");
            txtstream.WriteLine("}");

            txtstream.WriteLine("caption {");
            txtstream.WriteLine("        font-size: 48px;");
            txtstream.WriteLine("        color: #036;");
            txtstream.WriteLine("        font-weight: bolder;");
            txtstream.WriteLine("        font-variant: small-caps;");
            txtstream.WriteLine("}");

            txtstream.WriteLine("th {");
            txtstream.WriteLine("        font-size: 12px;");
            txtstream.WriteLine("        color: #FFF;");
            txtstream.WriteLine("        background-color: #06C;");
            txtstream.WriteLine("        padding: 8px 4px;");
            txtstream.WriteLine("        border-bottom: 1px solid #015ebc;");
            txtstream.WriteLine("}");

            txtstream.WriteLine("table {");
            txtstream.WriteLine("        margin: 0;");
```

```
txtstream.WriteLine("          padding: 0;");
txtstream.WriteLine("          border-collapse: collapse;");
txtstream.WriteLine("          border: 1px solid #06C;");
txtstream.WriteLine("          width: 100%");
txtstream.WriteLine("}");

txtstream.WriteLine("#itsthetable th a:link, #itsthetable th a:visited {");
txtstream.WriteLine("          color: #FFF;");
txtstream.WriteLine("          text-decoration: none;");
txtstream.WriteLine("          border-left: 5px solid #FFF;");
txtstream.WriteLine("          padding-left: 3px;");
txtstream.WriteLine("}");

txtstream.WriteLine("th a:hover, #itsthetable th a:active {");
txtstream.WriteLine("          color: #F90;");
txtstream.WriteLine("          text-decoration: line-through;");
txtstream.WriteLine("          border-left: 5px solid #F90;");
txtstream.WriteLine("          padding-left: 3px;");
txtstream.WriteLine("}");

txtstream.WriteLine("tbody th:hover {");
txtstream.WriteLine("          background-image:
url(imgs/tbody_hover.gif);");
txtstream.WriteLine("          background-position: bottom;");
txtstream.WriteLine("          background-repeat: repeat-x;");
txtstream.WriteLine("}");

txtstream.WriteLine("td {");
txtstream.WriteLine("          background-color: #f2f2f2;");
txtstream.WriteLine("          padding: 4px;");
txtstream.WriteLine("          font-size: 12px;");
txtstream.WriteLine("}");

txtstream.WriteLine("#itsthetable td:hover {");
txtstream.WriteLine("          background-color: #f8f8f8;");

txtstream.WriteLine("}");

txtstream.WriteLine("#itsthetable td a:link, #itsthetable td a:visited {");
txtstream.WriteLine("          color: #039;");
txtstream.WriteLine("          text-decoration: none;");
txtstream.WriteLine("          border-left: 3px solid #039;");
txtstream.WriteLine("          padding-left: 3px;");
txtstream.WriteLine("}");

txtstream.WriteLine("#itsthetable td a:hover, #itsthetable td a:active {");
txtstream.WriteLine("          color: #06C;");
txtstream.WriteLine("          text-decoration: line-through;");
txtstream.WriteLine("          border-left: 3px solid #06C;");
txtstream.WriteLine("          padding-left: 3px;");
```

```
txtstream.WriteLine("}");

txtstream.WriteLine("#itsthetable th {");
txtstream.WriteLine("        text-align: left;");
txtstream.WriteLine("        width: 150px;");
txtstream.WriteLine("}");

txtstream.WriteLine("#itsthetable tr {");
txtstream.WriteLine("        border-bottom: 1px solid #CCC;");
txtstream.WriteLine("}");

txtstream.WriteLine("#itsthetable thead th {");
txtstream.WriteLine("        background-image: url(imgs/thead_back.gif);");
txtstream.WriteLine("        background-repeat: repeat-x;");
txtstream.WriteLine("        background-color: #06C;");
txtstream.WriteLine("        height: 30px;");
txtstream.WriteLine("        font-size: 18px;");
txtstream.WriteLine("        text-align: center;");
txtstream.WriteLine("        text-shadow: #333 2px 2px;");
txtstream.WriteLine("        border: 2px;");
txtstream.WriteLine("}");

txtstream.WriteLine("#itsthetable tfoot th {");
txtstream.WriteLine("        background-image: url(imgs/tfoot_back.gif);");
txtstream.WriteLine("        background-repeat: repeat-x;");
txtstream.WriteLine("        background-color: #036;");
txtstream.WriteLine("        height: 30px;");
txtstream.WriteLine("        font-size: 28px;");
txtstream.WriteLine("        text-align: center;");
txtstream.WriteLine("        text-shadow: #333 2px 2px;");
txtstream.WriteLine("}");

txtstream.WriteLine("#itsthetable tfoot td {");
txtstream.WriteLine("        background-image: url(imgs/tfoot_back.gif);");
txtstream.WriteLine("        background-repeat: repeat-x;");
txtstream.WriteLine("        background-color: #036;");
txtstream.WriteLine("        color: FFF;");
txtstream.WriteLine("        height: 30px;");
txtstream.WriteLine("        font-size: 24px;");
txtstream.WriteLine("        text-align: left;");
txtstream.WriteLine("        text-shadow: #333 2px 2px;");
txtstream.WriteLine("}");

txtstream.WriteLine("tbody td a[href=\"http://www.csslab.cl/\"] {");
txtstream.WriteLine("        font-weight: bolder;");
txtstream.WriteLine("}");
txtstream.WriteLine("</style>");
txtstream.WriteLine("<body>");
txtstream.WriteLine("<center>");
txtstream.WriteLine("<table Style=\"Border:0;\">");
```

```
txtstream.WriteLine("<tr><TH Nowrap STYLE=\"background-
color:white;FONT-WEIGHT:normal; FONT-SIZE: 48px; COLOR: navy; FONT-STYLE:
normal; FONT-FAMILY: Edwardian Script ITC\"></TH></tr>");
        txtstream.WriteLine("</table>");
        txtstream.WriteLine("<table style=\"border:Double;border-
width:1px;border-color:navy;\" cellpadding=2 cellspacing=2 Width=0>");
        txtstream.WriteLine("<tr>");
        txtstream.WriteLine("    <th align=\"left\">ISAM NAME</th>");
        txtstream.WriteLine("</tr>");


        foreach (string v in vname)
        {

            txtstream.WriteLine("<tr>");
            txtstream.WriteLine("    <td align=\"left\">" + v + "</td>");
            txtstream.WriteLine("</tr>");

        }
        txtstream.WriteLine("</table>");
        txtstream.WriteLine("</body>");
        txtstream.WriteLine("</html>");
        txtstream.Close();


        webBrowser1.Navigate(System.Environment.CurrentDirectory +
"\\Registry.html");
    }

  }
}
```

Running the code above produces this:

ISAM NAME
dBase 5.0
dBase III
dBase IV
Excel 3.0
Excel 4.0
Excel 5.0
Excel 8.0
Exchange 4.0
HTML Export
HTML Import
Jet 2.x
Jet 3.x
Lotus WJ2
Lotus WJ3
Lotus WK1
Lotus WK3
Lotus WK4
Outlook 9.0
Paradox 3.x
Paradox 4.x
Paradox 5.x
Paradox 7.x
Text

Let's run this against the 3.5 ISAMS:

```csharp
using System;
using System.Collections.Generic;
using System.ComponentModel;
using System.Data;
using System.Drawing;
using System.Linq;
using System.Text;
using System.Threading.Tasks;
using System.Windows.Forms;
using Microsoft.Win32;
using Scripting;

namespace WindowsFormsApp4
{
    public partial class Form1 : Form
    {
        public Form1()
        {
            InitializeComponent();
        }

        private void Form1_Load(object sender, EventArgs e)
        {
            RegistryKey regKey =
Registry.LocalMachine.OpenSubKey("SOFTWARE\\WOW6432Node\\Microsoft\\Jet\\3
.5\\ISAM Formats");
            string[] vname = regKey.GetSubKeyNames();
            string name = "";
            string nk = "";
            string value = "";

            FileSystemObject fso = new FileSystemObject();
            TextStream txtstream =
fso.OpenTextFile(System.Environment.CurrentDirectory + "\\Registry.html",
IOMode.ForWriting, true, Tristate.TristateUseDefault);
            txtstream.WriteLine("<hmtl>");
            txtstream.WriteLine("<head>");
            txtstream.WriteLine("<title></title>");
            txtstream.WriteLine("<style type=text/css>");
            txtstream.WriteLine("#itsthetable {");
            txtstream.WriteLine("       font-family: Georgia, \"Times New Roman\",
Times, serif;");
            txtstream.WriteLine("       color: #036;");
            txtstream.WriteLine("}");

            txtstream.WriteLine("caption {");
            txtstream.WriteLine("       font-size: 48px;");
            txtstream.WriteLine("       color: #036;");
            txtstream.WriteLine("       font-weight: bolder;");
            txtstream.WriteLine("       font-variant: small-caps;");
```

```
txtstream.WriteLine("}");

txtstream.WriteLine("th {");
txtstream.WriteLine("        font-size: 12px;");
txtstream.WriteLine("        color: #FFF;");
txtstream.WriteLine("        background-color: #06C;");
txtstream.WriteLine("        padding: 8px 4px;");
txtstream.WriteLine("        border-bottom: 1px solid #015ebc;");
txtstream.WriteLine("}");

txtstream.WriteLine("table {");
txtstream.WriteLine("        margin: 0;");
txtstream.WriteLine("        padding: 0;");
txtstream.WriteLine("        border-collapse: collapse;");
txtstream.WriteLine("        border: 1px solid #06C;");
txtstream.WriteLine("        width: 100%");
txtstream.WriteLine("}");

txtstream.WriteLine("#itsthetable th a:link, #itsthetable th a:visited {");
txtstream.WriteLine("        color: #FFF;");
txtstream.WriteLine("        text-decoration: none;");
txtstream.WriteLine("        border-left: 5px solid #FFF;");
txtstream.WriteLine("        padding-left: 3px;");
txtstream.WriteLine("}");

txtstream.WriteLine("th a:hover, #itsthetable th a:active {");
txtstream.WriteLine("        color: #F90;");
txtstream.WriteLine("        text-decoration: line-through;");
txtstream.WriteLine("        border-left: 5px solid #F90;");
txtstream.WriteLine("        padding-left: 3px;");
txtstream.WriteLine("}");

txtstream.WriteLine("tbody th:hover {");
txtstream.WriteLine("        background-image:
url(imgs/tbody_hover.gif);");
txtstream.WriteLine("        background-position: bottom;");
txtstream.WriteLine("        background-repeat: repeat-x;");
txtstream.WriteLine("}");

txtstream.WriteLine("td {");
txtstream.WriteLine("        background-color: #f2f2f2;");
txtstream.WriteLine("        padding: 4px;");
txtstream.WriteLine("        font-size: 12px;");
txtstream.WriteLine("}");

txtstream.WriteLine("#itsthetable td:hover {");
txtstream.WriteLine("        background-color: #f8f8f8;");

txtstream.WriteLine("}");
```

```
txtstream.WriteLine("#itsthetable td a:link, #itsthetable td a:visited {");
txtstream.WriteLine("        color: #039;");
txtstream.WriteLine("        text-decoration: none;");
txtstream.WriteLine("        border-left: 3px solid #039;");
txtstream.WriteLine("        padding-left: 3px;");
txtstream.WriteLine("}");

txtstream.WriteLine("#itsthetable td a:hover, #itsthetable td a:active {");
txtstream.WriteLine("        color: #06C;");
txtstream.WriteLine("        text-decoration: line-through;");
txtstream.WriteLine("        border-left: 3px solid #06C;");
txtstream.WriteLine("        padding-left: 3px;");
txtstream.WriteLine("}");

txtstream.WriteLine("#itsthetable th {");
txtstream.WriteLine("        text-align: left;");
txtstream.WriteLine("        width: 150px;");
txtstream.WriteLine("}");

txtstream.WriteLine("#itsthetable tr {");
txtstream.WriteLine("        border-bottom: 1px solid #CCC;");
txtstream.WriteLine("}");

txtstream.WriteLine("#itsthetable thead th {");
txtstream.WriteLine("        background-image: url(imgs/thead_back.gif);");
txtstream.WriteLine("        background-repeat: repeat-x;");
txtstream.WriteLine("        background-color: #06C;");
txtstream.WriteLine("        height: 30px;");
txtstream.WriteLine("        font-size: 18px;");
txtstream.WriteLine("        text-align: center;");
txtstream.WriteLine("        text-shadow: #333 2px 2px;");
txtstream.WriteLine("        border: 2px;");
txtstream.WriteLine("}");

txtstream.WriteLine("#itsthetable tfoot th {");
txtstream.WriteLine("        background-image: url(imgs/tfoot_back.gif);");
txtstream.WriteLine("        background-repeat: repeat-x;");
txtstream.WriteLine("        background-color: #036;");
txtstream.WriteLine("        height: 30px;");
txtstream.WriteLine("        font-size: 28px;");
txtstream.WriteLine("        text-align: center;");
txtstream.WriteLine("        text-shadow: #333 2px 2px;");
txtstream.WriteLine("}");

txtstream.WriteLine("#itsthetable tfoot td {");
txtstream.WriteLine("        background-image: url(imgs/tfoot_back.gif);");
txtstream.WriteLine("        background-repeat: repeat-x;");
txtstream.WriteLine("        background-color: #036;");
txtstream.WriteLine("        color: FFF;");
txtstream.WriteLine("        height: 30px;");
```

```
txtstream.WriteLine("        font-size: 24px;");
txtstream.WriteLine("        text-align: left;");
txtstream.WriteLine("        text-shadow: #333 2px 2px;");
txtstream.WriteLine("}");

txtstream.WriteLine("tbody td a[href=\"http://www.csslab.cl/\"] {");
txtstream.WriteLine("        font-weight: bolder;");
txtstream.WriteLine("}");
txtstream.WriteLine("</style>");
txtstream.WriteLine("<body>");
txtstream.WriteLine("<center>");
txtstream.WriteLine("<table Style=\"Border:0;\">");
txtstream.WriteLine("<tr><TH Nowrap STYLE=\"background-
color:white;FONT-WEIGHT:normal; FONT-SIZE: 48px; COLOR: navy; FONT-STYLE:
normal; FONT-FAMILY: Edwardian Script ITC\"></TH></tr>");
txtstream.WriteLine("</table>");
txtstream.WriteLine("<table style=\"border:Double;border-
width:1px;border-color:navy;\" cellpadding=2 cellspacing=2 Width=0>");
txtstream.WriteLine("<tr>");
txtstream.WriteLine("    <th align=\"left\">ISAM NAME</th>");
txtstream.WriteLine("</tr>");


foreach (string v in vname)
{

    txtstream.WriteLine("<tr>");
    txtstream.WriteLine("    <td align=\"left\">" + v + "</td>");
    txtstream.WriteLine("</tr>");

}
txtstream.WriteLine("</table>");
txtstream.WriteLine("</body>");
txtstream.WriteLine("</html>");
txtstream.Close();


}
}
```

And the results:

Problem number two is do you really want to have to constantly have to work on the code every time a new type of entry is added that you can't use and filter that out, too.

Problem number three is do you really have the time to allow the code to do to create a DataGridView. In fact, unless you're dealing with a very specific and limited group of registry keys, going after 2000 ProgIDs and displaying them can prove to be a labor of disgust.

Simply put, the code logic is too slow to be worth doing that way.

It would be much intuitive if we created a read only replication of the registry where the user of the program can find the what he or she is looking for and then click through all the subkeys and see all the settings.

Besides, if the only thing you want to look at are the ProgIDs, creating a new Windows Form Application, making a reference to System.Management and then using the below code will give this view in less than 5 seconds:

```csharp
using System;
using System.Collections.Generic;
using System.ComponentModel;
using System.Data;
using System.Drawing;
using System.Linq;
using System.Text;
using System.Threading.Tasks;
using System.Windows.Forms;
using System.Management;
namespace WindowsFormsApp3
{
    public partial class Form1 : Form
    {
        public Form1()
        {
            InitializeComponent();
        }

        private void Form1_Load(object sender, EventArgs e)
        {
            ManagementClass mc = new ManagementClass();
            mc.Path.NamespacePath = "root\\cimv2";
            mc.Path.ClassName = "Win32_ClassicCOMClassSetting";
            ManagementObjectCollection moc = mc.GetInstances();
            foreach(ManagementObject mo in moc)
            {
                foreach (PropertyData prop in mo.Properties)
                {
                    if (prop.Name == "ProgId")
                    {
                        if(prop.Value != null)
                        {
                            listBox1.Items.Add(prop.Value);
                        }

                    }
                }
```

```
                    }
               listBox1.Sorted = true;
             }
           }
       }
```

The visual:

As you can see, we can get quite granular with what we are looking for in the registry. But at the cost of speed and end user patience.

But if you could reward them with visuals and control over manipulating the information, then, perhaps the end user might stop arguing about it and realize you were, indeed, providing him or her with a quality product.

WORKING WITH

REGISTRY VALUE TYPES

The art of code logic selection

If you've been working with Microsoft's products for some time, you've come to realize that there's always more than one way to accomplish a task. Working code to acquire information from the registry is no exception.

Point in case is how you deal with registry data types. What the .Net Framework calls ValueKinds. In plain English, these data types consists of 6 types, 3 are strings, one is binary and two are WORDS. These describe:

> REG_SZ
> REG_EXPAND_SZ
> REG_MULTI_SZ
> REG_DWORD
> REG_QWORD
> REG_BINARY

There are two ways of working with these types. The way I learned how to logically handle each one by code or use the built-in functionality of a class that simply does it for you.

Now, you've already seen my logic dealing with parsing and it is based on how I knew how to decipher them. Back when I was wrapping my head around how to deal with them – with little to no documentation, it was mostly trial and error. With a lot of keyboards being replaced due to temperament issues.

By the time I finally got the logic right, .Net came out and turn hell into heavenly ease.

When you acquire a list of ValueNames, you pair that with a list of ValueKinds. Let's lay that track out first:

```
private void Form1_Load(object sender, EventArgs e)
{

    String rv = "";
    String regkind = "";
    String[] VNames =
Registry.LocalMachine.OpenSubKey("System\\CurrentControlSet\\Cont
rol\\Session Manager").GetValueNames();
    RegistryValueKind[] ValueKinds =
Registry.LocalMachine.OpenSubKey("System\\CurrentControlSet\\Cont
rol\\Session Manager").GetValueKinds();

    int x = 0;
    foreach (RegistryValueKind vk in ValueKinds)
    {

        String Vn = VNames.GetValue(x).ToString();
        x = x + 1;

        switch (vk)
        {
            case RegistryValueKind.String:
                {
                    regkind="REG_SZ";

                    break;
                }
            case RegistryValueKind.ExpandString:
                {
                    regkind="REG_EXPAND_SZ";
```

```
                    break;
                }
            case RegistryValueKind.MultiString:
                {
                    regkind="REG_MULTI_SZ";

                    break;
                }
            case RegistryValueKind.DWord:
                {
                    regkind="REG_DWORD";

                    break;
                }
            case RegistryValueKind.QWord:
                {
                    regkind="REG_QWORD";

                    break;
                }
            case RegistryValueKind.Binary:
                {
                    regkind="REG_BINARY";

                    break;
                }
        }
        if (Vn == "")
        {
            Vn = "(Default)";
        }
    }
}
```

At this point, as you can see, we've created a group of empty sub routines we're going to need to work. You can also see where the ValueNames collection is index to marry up with the enumeration of the ValueKinds and at the end of the if the string name – Vn – is empty, it is replaced with "(Default)".

This is done because we need the ValueName to make the call to get the value and in order to do that correctly, we need to be able to use the ValueKind's value to decide how we're going to deal with its value.

DEALING WITH REGISTRY NAMEVALUES

Working with REG_SZ and REG_EXPAND_SZ:

```
                case RegistryValueKind.String:
                    {
                        regkind = "REG_SZ";
                        string rv =
Registry.LocalMachine.OpenSubKey("System\\CurrentControlSet\\Cont
rol\\Session Manager").GetValue(Vn).ToString();
                        break;
                    }
                case RegistryValueKind.ExpandString:
                    {
                        regkind = "REG_EXPAND_SZ";
                        string rv =
Registry.LocalMachine.OpenSubKey("System\\CurrentControlSet\\Cont
rol\\Session Manager").GetValue(Vn).ToString();
                        break;
                    }
```

Working with REG_MULTI_SZ:

```
                case RegistryValueKind.MultiString:
                    {

                        string[] tempstr =
(string[])Registry.LocalMachine.OpenSubKey("System\\CurrentContro
lSet\\Control\\Session Manager").GetValue(Vn);

                        regkind = "REG_MULTI_SZ";
                        String value = "";
                        for (int i = 0; i <
tempstr.GetLength(0); i++)
                        {
                            if (value != "")
                            {
                                value = value + ", ";
                            }
```

```
                                value = value +
tempstr.GetValue(i).ToString();
                                }
                                rv = value;
```

Working with REG_DWORD and REG_QWORD:

```
                    case RegistryValueKind.DWord:
                        {
                            regkind = "REG_DWORD";

                            int l =
(int)Registry.LocalMachine.OpenSubKey("System\\CurrentControlSet\
\Control\\Session Manager").GetValue(Vn);
                            rv = "(0x" + l.ToString("X8") + ") "
+ l.ToString();

                            break;
                        }
                    case RegistryValueKind.QWord:
                        {

                            regkind = "REG_QWORD";
                            int l =
(int)Registry.LocalMachine.OpenSubKey("System\\CurrentControlSet\
\Control\\Session Manager").GetValue(Vn);
                            rv = "(0x" + l.ToString("X8") + ") "
+ l.ToString();

                            break;
                        }
```

Working with REG_BINARY:

```
                    case RegistryValueKind.Binary:
                        {
                            byte[] bi =
(byte[])Registry.LocalMachine.OpenSubKey("System\\CurrentControlS
et\\Control\\Session Manager").GetValue(Vn);
                            regkind = "REG_BINARY";
                            string tempstr = "";
                            string value = "";
                            int len = bi.Length;
                            for (int i = 0; i < len; i++)
                            {
                                tempstr = bi[i].ToString("x");
                                if (tempstr.Length == 1)
```

```
                            {
                                tempstr = "0" + tempstr;
                            }
                            value = value + tempstr + " ";
                            tempstr = "";
                        }
                        rv = value;
                        break;
                }
```

When we get at the end of the loop, we want to do something with the information. That, of course, could be almost anything you want it to be. From adding the information to a database, a csv file, ASP, ASPX, XML and my favorite HTML. All of these outputs would create a temporary or permanent file which could later be worked into a comparison program to see if something changed that should have.

As for the alternative ways of dealing with the values, you could include the WMI StdRegProv, have it go to the same location in the registry and use its – I know what to do - attitude to make the call for each specific registry datatype. These functions include:

```
GetStringValue
GetExpandedStringValue
GetMultiStringValue
GetDWORDValue
GetBinaryValue
```

But you are still going to have to work the return values into the way it is seen in the registry. In truth, what these are really good for is when you have a known key with a known value that you want to work with on either your local machine or on a remote machine.

Whatever way you want to accomplish what needs to be done, the bigger picture is it can be done in more ways than one.

This code using C#.Net works to connect to a remote registry, too.

```csharp
            ConnectionOptions cops = new ConnectionOptions();
            cops.Authentication =
AuthenticationLevel.PacketPrivacy;
            cops.Impersonation = ImpersonationLevel.Impersonate;
            cops.Locale = "MS_0409";
            cops.Username = "Administrator";
            cops.Password = "*************";

            ManagementPath path = new ManagementPath();
            path.ClassName = "StdRegProv";
            path.NamespacePath = "root\\default";
            path.Server = "WIN-7JBE1NVOJBF";

            ManagementScope scope = new ManagementScope(path,
cops);
            scope.Connect();

        }
```

ALTERNATIVE WAYS TO WRITE REGISTRY CODE

The purpose of this code is to show you how you can create alternative code using the .Net framework or COM to accomplish similar tasks. Windows Management Instrumentation (WMI) has a class that can be used to perform much of the same functionality that Microsoft.Win32 namespace enables you to do.

Below, is a list of methods you can use when creating a connection to this class:

```
CheckAccess
CreateKey
DeleteKey
DeleteValue

EnumKey
EnumValues

GetBinaryValue
GetDWORDValue
GetExpandedStringValue
GetMultiStringValue
GetQWORDValue
GetStringValue

SetBinaryValue
SetDWORDValue
SetExpandedStringValue
SetMultiStringValue
SetQWORDValue
SetStringValue

GetSecurityDescriptor
SetSecurityDescriptor
```

Short of actually opening a specific key, which, if you think about it is really a pointless method considering you're actually either trying to enumerate through subkeys or attempting to retrieve a value, the WMI Provider does one thing the Microsoft.Win32 namespace doesn't let you do. Connect to a remote machine with username and password. Take a look at the code below. You will see exactly what I am talking about.

```
ConnectionOptions cops = new ConnectionOptions();
cops.Authentication = AuthenticationLevel.PacketPrivacy;
cops.Impersonation = ImpersonationLevel.Impersonate;
cops.Locale = "MS_0409";
cops.Username = "UserName";
cops.Password = "Password";

ManagementPath path = new ManagementPath();
path.ClassName = "StdRegProv";
path.NamespacePath = "root\\default";
path.Server = "192.168.0.99";

ManagementScope scope = new ManagementScope(path, cops);
scope.Connect();

ManagementClass mc = new ManagementClass();
mc.Path.NamespacePath = path.NamespacePath;
mc.Path.ClassName = path.ClassName;
ManagementBaseObject inparams = mc.GetMethodParameters("EnumKey");
inparams["hDefKey"] = 2147483650;
inparams["sSubKeyName"] = "SOFTWARE\\WOW6432Node\\Classes\\CLSID";
ManagementBaseObject retval = mc.InvokeMethod("EnumKey", inparams, null);
string[] names = (string[])retval.Properties["sNames"].Value;
Console.Out.WriteLine(names.GetLength(0));
```

So does this:

```
SWbemLocator L = new SWbemLocator();
SWbemServices svc = L.ConnectServer("192.168.0.99", "root\\Default", "UserName", "Password", "MS-0409");
SWbemObject obj = svc.Get("StdRegProv", 0, null);

int v = 0;
SWbemObject inparams = obj.Methods_.Item("EnumKey").InParameters;
inparams.Properties_.Item("hDefKey", 0).set_Value(0x80000002);
inparams.Properties_.Item("sSubKeyName",
0).set_Value("SOFTWARE\\WOW6432Node\\Classes\\CLSID");
SWbemObject outParams = obj.ExecMethod_("EnumKey", inparams);
Object[] names = outParams.Properties_.Item("sNames").get_Value();
Console.Out.WriteLine(names.GetLength(0));
```

So, yes, it is WMI and yes, it will let you check to see if your credentials work and yes, you can't pass credentials using Microsoft.Win32.

With that said, which one should you really be using when you can prove there is a permissions issue that someone else needs to fix and not your code you know won't work and make you look like an incompetent fool?

In the next book, we're going to be using the WMI StdRegProv class extensively and show you how you can connect using a secure string to make it almost impossible for someone to figure it out.

Have a Merry Christmas!

www.ingramcontent.com/pod-product-compliance
Lightning Source LLC
Chambersburg PA
CBHW031244050326
40690CB00007B/947